FALL SEVEN TIMES
TIMES
STAND UP
EIGHT

Copyright © 2015 by John Mason

ISBN 978-1-61795-530-3

Published by Worthy Inspired, an imprint of Worthy Publishing Group, a division of Worthy Media, Inc., One Franklin Park, 6100 Tower Circle, Suite 210, Franklin, TN 37067.

Mason, John, 1955-
Fall seven times stand up eight : how to succeed no matter what / by John Mason.
pages cm
ISBN 978-1-61795-530-3 (hardcover)
1. Success—Religious aspects—Christianity. 2. Christian life. I. Title.
BV4598.3.M3737 2015
248.4—dc23

2015008626

Cover Design by Micah Kandros

Printed in the United States of America

1 2 3 4 5—LBM—19 18 17 16 15

JOHN
MASON

FALL SEVEN TIMES
TIMES
STAND UP
EIGHT

HOW TO SUCCEED
NO MATTER WHAT

WORTHY®
Inspired

INTRODUCTION

I've had the privilege of knowing many successful people over my lifetime, and from them I've learned a lot. I remember when I first spent time with these people and got to know them better how surprised I was by the number of failures they had. Still, their failures didn't defeat them but in most cases inspired them and pushed them to greater success. They got back up smarter and more determined than ever. You can too. It's one of the reasons I've written this book, *Fall Seven Times Stand Up Eight*.

We all experience failure and make mistakes. In fact, successful people have more failures than average people do. I've found it is better to fail in doing *something* than to excel at doing *nothing*. A flawed diamond is more valuable than a perfect brick.

God isn't surprised by your stumbles. His love, grace, mercy, and forgiveness are bigger than any mess you make. He never sees any of us as failures; He only sees us as learners. We fail when we don't learn from each experience. The decision is up to us—we can choose to turn a failure into a hitching post or a guidepost in our lives. Let this book direct you as you make your way back up.

LOOKING INWARD

CHAPTER 1

ARE YOU STUMBLING TOWARD AN UNCERTAIN FUTURE?

My friend, the late Myles Munroe said, "There is something for you to start that is ordained for you to finish." God made you special for a purpose. He has an assignment for you to do no one else can do as well as you can. Out of billions of applicants, you're the most qualified. You have the right combination of what it takes. God has given each person the measure of faith to do what He's called him or her to do. Every person is gifted.

A person is never what he ought to be until he is doing what he ought to be doing.

God holds us not only responsible for what we have, but for what we could have; not only for what we are, but for what we might be.

"The height of your accomplishments will equal the depth of your convictions. Seek happiness for its own sake, and you will not find it; seek for purpose, and happiness will follow as a shadow comes with the sunshine."

William Scolavino

As you reach for your purpose, it will be like a magnet that pulls you, not like a brass ring that only goes around once. Destiny draws.

John Foster said, "It is a poor disgraceful thing not to be able to reply, with some degree of certainty, to the simple questions, 'What will you be? What will you do?'"

Dr. Charles Garfield added, "Peak performers are people who are committed to a compelling mission. It is very clear that they care deeply about what they do and their efforts, energies and enthusiasms are traceable back to that particular mission."

You're not truly free until you've been made captive by your supreme mission in life.

Don't just pray that God will do this or that, rather pray that God will make His purpose known to you.

William Cowper said, "The only true happiness comes from squandering ourselves for a purpose."

When you base your life on principle, 99% of your decisions are already made.

Psalm 138:8 reads, "The LORD will fulfill his purpose for me; thy steadfast love, O LORD, endures for ever" (RSV).

As individuals go their right way, destiny accompanies them.

Know that God is with you and will provide what you need to accomplish your purpose. The God who made the mouth will also provide the food.

Don't part company with your purpose. It is an anchor in the storm.

Man is responsible to God for becoming what God has made possible for him to become.

A purposeless life is an early death.

Rick Renner commented, "The only thing that will keep you from the will of God is if you look at yourself and say, 'I'm not so much among so many.' "

You can't do anything about the length of your life, but you can do something about its width and depth.

What you believe is the force that determines what you accomplish or fail to accomplish in life.

Too many people know what they are running from, but not what they are running to.

Take care of your purpose and the end will take care of itself.

You can predict your future by the awareness you have of your purpose.

First, concentrate on finding your purpose, then focus on fulfilling it.

Purpose, not money, is your real asset.

What you set your heart on will determine how you'll spend your life.

A person going nowhere can be sure of reaching his destination.

Considering an action? Listen to Marcus Aurelius: "Without a purpose nothing should be done."

Robert Byrne said, "The purpose of life is a life of purpose."

Martin Luther King Jr. said, "If a man hasn't discovered something that he will die for, he isn't fit to live."

Abandon yourself to destiny.

CHAPTER 2

HAVE THE COURAGE TO LIVE. ANYONE CAN QUIT.

A few years back at a conference we both spoke at in Hawaii, I had the opportunity to talk to Peter Lowe, the founder of the successful Get Motivated Seminars. As we talked, he commented, "The most common trait I have found in all people that are successful is that they have conquered the temptation to give up." One of the best ways to give your best a chance is to rise when you're knocked down.

As an author, I have the privilege of signing many books. I like to write encouraging expressions in each book before I sign my name. One of my most frequent encouragements is: Never give up!

"The world will always give you the opportunity to quit, but only the world would call quitting an opportunity" (Clint Brown). In trying times, too many people quit trying. The choice of giving up or going on is a defining moment in your life.

Too many people stop faster than they start. Instead of stopping, follow this English proverb: "Don't fall before you are pushed."

More than twenty-five years ago, I remember feeling led to write.

I didn't know what to do. I knew over 1,000 new books are published each day. I knew that 70% of all books are never read.

If you had asked me to list fifty things I would do in college, writing a book wouldn't have been one of them. But, I started . . . and I worked at it for nearly two years.

I had no built-in audience, no A's in English (mostly B's and C's). But I did have determination and a commitment to finish. After almost two years, I'll never forget at 4:30 in the morning typing the last word into my Apple IIC computer (128K) falling into my bed sobbing for quite a while . . . it was finished.

My first book, *An Enemy Called Average,* was done. Little did I know more than 600,000 people were about to read that book in more than thirty languages around the world.

That's one book each mile at the equator around the world twenty-five times!

I promise you this . . . You will be shocked at the impact of your persistence.

The choice is simple. You can either stand up and count or lie down and be counted out. Defeat never comes to people until they admit it. Your success will be measured by your courage to keep on trying.

A lazy man is always judged by what he doesn't do. The choice of giving up or going on is a defining moment in your life. You cannot turn back the clock. But you can wind it up again.

One person with commitment, persistence and endurance will always accomplish more than a thousand people with just an interest.

The person who wants to do something finds a way; the other finds an excuse.

Joel Budd remarked, "It isn't the final say so, unless you say so."

Richard Nixon mused, "A man is not finished when he is defeated. He is finished when he quits."

Your success begins where most others quit. Pay particular attention to when people give up . . . that's your best opportunity.

The famous boxer, Archie Moore, reflected, "If I don't get off the mat, I'll lose the fight." Nobody and nothing can keep you down unless you decide not to rise again. H. E. Jansen said, "The man who wins may have been counted out several times, but he didn't hear the referee." Find a way *to,* not a way *not to.*

Margaret Thatcher understood the principle of not quitting when she advised, "You may have to fight a battle more than once to win it."

"I can't!" is the conclusion of fools. Listen to Clare Booth Luce: "There are no hopeless situations; there are only men who have grown hopeless about them."

Admiral Chester Nimitz remarked, "God grant me the courage not to give up what I think is right even though I think it is hopeless." Giving up is the ultimate tragedy.

Quitting and failure always begin with alibis, justification, and feeling sorry for yourself.

David Zucker added, "Quit now, you'll never make it. If you disregard this advice, you'll be halfway there."

CHAPTER 3

DON'T JUMP INTO TROUBLE
MOUTH FIRST.

Sometime your biggest enemies and most trustworthy friends are the words you say to yourself. Choose to speak positive, motivating, kind words. Pascal commented, "Kind words do not cost much. They never blister the tongue or lips. Mental trouble was never known to arise from such quarters. Though they do not cost much, yet they accomplish much. They bring out the good nature in others. They also produce their own image in a man's soul, and what a beautiful picture it is."

Take a tip from nature—your ears aren't made to shut, but your mouth is! When an argument flares up, the wise man quenches it with silence. Sometimes you have to be quiet to be heard.

Recently I saw a sign under a mounted large-mouth bass. It read: "If I had kept my mouth shut I wouldn't be here." How true! What we say is important.

Let me pose this question for you: What would happen if you changed what you said about your biggest problem, your biggest opportunity?

Colossians 4:6 counsels, "Let your speech be alway with grace, seasoned with salt, that ye may know how ye ought to answer every man."

Never let your tongue say what your head must pay for later.

Johann Lavater said, "Never tell evil of a man if you do not know it for certain and if you know it for certain, then ask yourself, 'Why should I tell it?'"

Our prayer to God ought to be, "Oh Lord, please fill my mouth with worthwhile stuff, and nudge me when I've said enough."

Proverbs 29:11 says, "A fool uttereth all his mind."

Always speak less than you know.

The human tongue is only a few inches from the brain, but when you listen to some people talk, they seem miles apart. The tongue runs fastest when the brain is in neutral.

"Impossible," Napoleon is quoted as saying, "is a word found only in the dictionary of fools." What words are in your dictionary?

Don't jump into trouble mouth first. Choose your words carefully. Most of the time the less said the better. The more words you says the greater the likelihood you'll have to eat some of them later. You can say more by saying less.

A man joined a monastery in which the monks were allowed to speak only two words every seven years. After the first seven years had passed, the new monk met with the abbot, who asked him, "Well, what are your two words?"

"Food's bad," replied the man, who then went back to his silence.

Seven years later the clergyman asked, "What are your two words now?"

"Bed's hard," the man responded.

Seven years later—twenty-one years after his initial entry into the monastery—the man met with the abbot for the third and final time. "And what are your two words this time?" the abbot asked.

"I quit."

"Well, I'm not surprised," the cleric answered disgustedly. "All you've done since you got here is complain!"

"The words 'I am' are potent words; be careful what you hitch them to. What you're claiming has a way of reaching back and claiming you."

A. L. Kietselman

Job 6:25 reminds us: "How forcible are right words!"

The Bible says there are life and death in the power of the tongue (Proverbs 18:21). What words have the most powerful effect on you? George Burnham said, "'I can't do it' never accomplished anything. 'I will try' has performed wonders."

If your lips would keep from slips;
Five things observe with care;
To whom you speak, of whom you speak,
And how, and when, and where.

W. E. Norris

Sir Wilfred Grenfell said, "Start some kind word on its travels. There is no telling where the good it may do will stop."

What about the words we tell ourselves? The most important person you talk to all day is you. So, be careful what you say to you.

CHAPTER 4

BE WHO YOU ARE.

Years ago I worked for a very successful man and self-made multi-millionaire. Not only was he doing well; he was also a very "unique" individual. This is something you notice quite quickly once you get to know him. It didn't take me very long to see a connection between his success and his distinctiveness.

I'll never forget one day talking with him and telling him how "different" he was. His response at first was quite negative. "What do you mean I'm different?" He, like most people, thought being called unique/different was negative.

Fortunately, I had a good working relationship with this boss. So, I could candidly explain to him what I meant and why what I said was a good thing. I told him that his "differentness" was a substantial asset for him and how nearly every highly successful person I know stands out and doesn't blend in.

Well, his eyes lit up, and his countenance changed the more I "complimented" him on his strangeness . . . in a good way.

I've always said one of the highest compliments you can hear is when someone says to you, "You're different!" You must be doing something unique, matchless, and even rare to hear those words.

Of course, I'm not encouraging you to be bizarre, nutty or weird. What I am saying is as you become you . . . you will stand out. So many people are just copies.

William Boetecher declared: "The more you learn what to do with yourself, and the more you do for others, the more you will learn to enjoy the abundant life."

I can spend large segments of time in airports because I frequently travel. Almost invariably when in an airport, I notice scores of people who look like they are in a hurry to nowhere. Isn't it incredible that so many people devote their whole lives to fields of endeavor that have nothing to do with the gifts and talents that God has given them? Incredibly, many spend their entire lives trying to change the way God made them.

God knew what He was doing when He put particular gifts, talents and strengths inside of you. 1 Corinthians 7:7 asserts, "Each man has his own gift from God" (NIV). Marcus Aurelieus said, "Take full account of the excellencies which you possess and in gratitude remember how you would hanker after them if you had them not."

Nathaniel Emmons said, "One principle reason men are so often useless is that they neglect their profession or calling and divide and shift their attention among a multitude of objects and pursuits." The best will always arise within you when you tap into the best gifts God has put in you.

William Matthews said, "One well cultivated talent, deepened and enlarged, is worth 100 shallow faculties."

Too many people take only their wants into consideration, never their talents and abilities. Deep down inside, if you are a musician, then make music. If you are a teacher, teach. Be what you are, and you will be at peace with yourself.

Do what's most natural for you. Yoruba said, "You can't stop a pig from wallowing in the mud."

"Ninety percent of the world's woe comes from people not knowing themselves, their abilities, their frailties and even their real virtues."

Sydney Harris

Abraham Lincoln mused, "Whatever you are, be a good one."

Robert Quillen reflected, "If you count all your assets you always show a profit."

Never judge yourself by your weaknesses. It was Malcolm Forbes, who claimed: "Too many people overvalue what they are not and undervalue what they are." You are richer than you think you are.

God loves you just the way you are, but He loves you too much to leave you the way you are. He wants you to use what is inside you. Stand out—don't blend in. Don't copy others and be a mynah bird.

"How glorious it is and also how painful—to be an exception." Billy Wilder adds, "Trust your instinct. Your mistakes might as well be your own, instead of someone else's."

Seize the opportunities to use your gifts. "Put yourself on view. This always brings your talents to light" (Baltasar Gracian).

Leaders are like eagles; they don't flock, and you find them one at a time. Be above mediocre . . . be an eagle. "Eagles commonly fly alone; the crows, daws, and starlings fly together" (John Webster).

E. E. Cummings advised, "To be nobody but yourself—in a world which is doing its best, night and day, to make you everybody else—means to fight the hardest battle which any human being can fight and never stop fighting." Be yourself—who else is better qualified?

CHAPTER 5

YOUR CHARACTER BECOMES YOUR LEGACY.

Every day we should ask ourselves, "Why should my boss/client hire me instead of someone else?" or "Why should people do business with me instead of my competitors?"

"Watch your actions; they become habits. Watch your habits; they become character. Watch your character; it becomes your destiny."

Frank Outlaw

Living a double life will get you nowhere twice as fast.

Character is the real foundation of all worthwhile success.

A good question to ask yourself is, "What kind of world would this world be if everybody were just like me?"

You are simply a book telling the world about its author.

"There is an infinite difference between a little wrong and just right, between fairly good and the best, between mediocrity and superiority," said Orison Swett Marden.

John Morely remarked, "No man can climb out beyond the limitations of his own character."

✓ Never be ashamed of doing right.

It takes less time to do something right than it does to explain why you did it wrong.

Character is something you either have or are.

Some people try to make something for themselves. Others try to make something of themselves.

Tryon Edwards said, "Thoughts lead on to purposes; purposes go forth in action; actions form habits; habits decide character, and character fixes our destiny."

✓ The Bible asserts in Proverbs 22:1, "A good name is rather to be chosen than great riches."

To change your character, you must begin at the control center—the heart. Spiritual bankruptcy is inevitable when a man is no longer able to keep the interest paid on his moral obligations. Men of power are feared, but only men of character are trusted.

Marcus Aurelius exhorted, "Never esteem as of advantage to thee that which shall make thee break thy word or lose thy self-respect."

W. J. Dawson counseled, "You need not choose evil, but only to fail to choose good, and you drift fast enough towards evil. You do not need to say, 'I will be bad,' you only have to say, 'I will not choose God's way,' and the choice of evil is settled."

There is no such thing as a necessary evil.

Phillip Brooks said, "A man who lives right and is right has more power in his silence than another has by his words."

Many a man's reputation would not recognize his character if they met in the dark.

Henry Ward Beecher said, "No man can tell whether he is rich or poor by turning to his ledger. It is the heart that makes a man rich. He is rich according to what he is, not according to what he has."

The traffic sign preaches the world's shortest sermon: Keep Right.

Let me pose this question for you: Would the boy you were be proud of the man you are?

Live so that your friends can defend you, but never have to do so. Consider what Woodrow Wilson said: "If you think about what you ought to do for people, your character will take care of itself."

It's hard to climb high when your character is low.

CHAPTER 6

DON'T BE YOUR OWN WORST ENEMY.

The great evangelist Dwight L. Moody said, "I've never met a man who gave me as much trouble as myself."

Follow the advice of my good friend, Dave Blunt; "Stay out of your own way!"

Ralph Waldo Emerson said, "It is impossible for man to be cheated by anyone but himself."

Gain control of your mind or it will gain control of you.

Your imagination dictates your openness to a positive direction.

As Norman Vincent Peale remarked, "Do not build up obstacles in your imagination. Remind yourself that God is with you and that nothing can defeat Him."

No one can defeat you unless you first defeat yourself. Self-image sets the boundaries and limits of each of our individual accomplishments. Charles Colton said, "We are sure to be losers when we quarrel with ourselves; it is civil war."

"Our best friends and our worst enemies are the thoughts we have about ourselves."

Dr. Frank Crane

Stop looking only at where you are and start looking at what you can be.

Be aware of your thoughts. They soon become words and actions very soon after that.

Wrong thinking almost always leads to misery.

Most of the stumbling blocks people complain about are under their hats.

Louis XIV commented, "There is little that can withstand a man who can conquer himself."

The Bible's wisdom counsels, "He that hath no rule over his own spirit is like a city that is broken down, and without walls" (Proverbs 25:28).

If you doubt yourself, listen to Alexander Dumas: "A person who doubts himself is like a man who enlists in the ranks of his enemy and bears arms against himself."

Tim Redmond observed, "Don't commit treason against your life and purpose."

"Your future depends on many things, but mostly on you."

Frank Tyger

Remember you are your own doctor when it comes to curing cold feet, a hot head, and a stuffy attitude.

"Our business in life is not to get ahead of others, but to get ahead of ourselves—to break our own records, to outstrip our yesterdays by today, to do our work with more force than ever before."

Stewart Johnson

If you would like to know who is responsible for most of your troubles, take a look in the mirror.

If you could kick the fellow responsible for most of your problems, you wouldn't be able to sit down for three weeks.

Your world first exists within you. Marriane Crawford said, "Every man carries with him the world in which he must live."

Zig Ziglar observes, "What you picture in your mind, your mind will go to work to accomplish. When you change your pictures, you automatically change your performance."

Amazingly, sometimes what you think is your greatest weakness can become a wonderful strength. Take, for example, the story of one ten-year-old boy who decided to study judo despite the fact that he had lost his left arm in a devastating car accident.

The boy began lessons with an old Japanese judo master. The boy was doing well, so he couldn't understand why, after three months of training, the master had taught him only one move.

"Sensei," the boy finally said, "shouldn't I be learning more moves?"

"This is the only move you know, but this is the only move you'll ever need to know," the sensei replied. Not quite understanding, but believing in his teacher, the boy kept training. Several months later, the sensei took the boy to his first tournament.

Surprising himself, the boy easily won his first two matches. The third match proved to be more difficult, but after some time, his opponent became impatient and charged; the boy deftly used his one move to win the match. Still amazed by his success, the boy was now in the finals.

This time, his opponent was bigger, stronger, and more experienced. For a while, the boy appeared to be overmatched. Concerned that the boy might get hurt, the referee called a time-out. He was about to stop the match when the sensei intervened.

"No," the sensei insisted, "let him continue."

Soon after the match resumed, his opponent made a critical mistake: He dropped his guard. Instantly, the boy used his move to pin him. The boy had won the match and the tournament. He was the champion.

On the way home, the boy and the sensei reviewed every move in each and every match. Then the boy summoned the courage to ask what was on his mind.

"Sensei, how did I win the tournament with only one move?"

"You win for two reasons," the Sensei answered. "First, you've almost mastered one of the most difficult throws in all of judo. And second, the only known defense for that move is for your opponent to grab your left arm."

The boy's biggest weakness had become his biggest strength.

You may succeed if nobody else believes in you, but you will never succeed if you don't believe in yourself.

Whatever you attach consistently to the words "I am," you will become.

CHAPTER 7

BETTER TO FAIL IN DOING SOMETHING THAN TO EXCEL IN DOING NOTHING.

A flawed diamond is always more valuable than a perfect brick.

When you're determined, you know it and so does everyone else.

You don't drown by falling in the water. You drown by staying there.

Get up! "For though a righteous man falls seven times, he rises again, but the are brought down by calamity." (Proverbs 24:16, NIV).

Good things come to those who go after them.

Perseverance is the result of a strong will. Stubbornness is the outcome of a strong won't.

Herbert Caufman adds, "Spurts don't count. The final score makes no mention of a splendid start if the finish proves that you were 'an also ran.'"

Montesquieu said, "Success often depends on knowing how long it will take to succeed."

Do you want to achieve something in life? Be like the stone-cutter. Jacob Riis says, "Look at the stone cutter hammering away at the rock, perhaps a 100 times without as much as a crack showing in it. At the 101st blow, it will split in two, and I know it was not the last blow that did it, but all that had gone before."

The secret of success: never let down and never let up.

Many times success consists of hanging on one minute longer.

"To finish first you must first finish," says champions race car driver Rick Mears.

Joel Hause said, "You may be whatever you resolve to be. Determine to be something in the world, and you will be something. 'I cannot' never accomplished anything; 'I will try' has wrought wonders."

Joseph Ross said, "It takes time to succeed because success is merely the natural reward of taking time to do anything well."

Revelation 2:10 says, "Be thou faithful unto death, and I will give thee a crown of life."

Keep in mind the words of Hamilton Holt: "Nothing worthwhile comes easily. Half effort does not produce half results. It produces no results. Work, continuous work, and hard work are the only way to accomplish results that last."

Persistence prevails when all else fails.

The truth is that persistence is a bitter plant, but it has sweet fruit.

Calvin Coolidge said, "'Press on' has solved and always will solve the problems of the human race."

James 5:11 reads, "Behold, we count them happy which endure."

Ecclesiastes declares, "Better is the end of a thing than the beginning thereof: and the patient in spirit is better than the proud in spirit" (7:8).

Persistence is the quality that is most needed when it is exhausted. Successful people go from failure to failure to failure until success is theirs.

Ralph Waldo Emerson said, "The great majority of men are bundles of beginnings."

All spiritual progress is like an unfolding vegetable bud. You first have a leading, then peace, then conviction, as the plant has root, bud, and fruit. Compte de Buffon says, "Never think that God's delays are God's denials. Hold on; hold fast; hold out. Patience is genius."

You will find that persistent people always have this attitude: they never lose the game; they just run out of time.

Victory always comes to the most persevering.

I agree with Charles Kettering when he said, "Keep on going and the chances are you will stumble on something perhaps when you are least expecting it."

No one finds life worth living. One must make it worth living.

Often genius is just another way of spelling persistence.

CHAPTER 8

WHEN YOU'RE GOOD AT MAKING EXCUSES, IT'S HARD TO BE GOOD AT ANYTHING ELSE.

Most people could learn from their mistakes if they weren't so busy denying and defending them.

"It seems these days that people who admit they're wrong get a lot further than people who prove they're right."

Deryl Pfizer

What poison is to food, alibis are to a productive life.

"Work brings profit; talk brings poverty!"

Proverbs 14:23, TLB

"Some men have thousands of reasons why they can't do what they want to do, when all they really need is one reason why they can."

Willis Whitney

Find a reason you can.

When you use excuses, you give up your power to change.

Our mistakes fail in their mission of helping us when we blame them on other people.

When it comes to excuses, the world is full of great inventors. Some spend half their lives telling what they are going to do, and the other half explaining why they didn't do it. An alibi reveals what you didn't do, hoping others will think you didn't do what you did.

Eliminate all your alibis. Excuses are an appalling waste of creative energy; you can't build on it. It's only good for wallowing in. The truth is a thousand alibis do not pay one debt.

Live your life, so your tombstone reads "No regrets."

When a winner makes a mistake, he says, "I was wrong." When a loser makes a mistake, he says, "It wasn't my fault." Do you admit and say "I was wrong," or do you say "It wasn't my fault." A winner explains; a loser explains away.

You can fail many times but not be a failure until you begin to blame someone else.

One who makes a mistake, and then makes an excuse for it, is making two mistakes. Note this truth: "The fox condemns the trap, not himself" (Blake). Don't find yourself talking like that old fox!

Time wasted thinking up excuses and alibis would always be better spent praying, planning, preparing and working toward your goals in life.

You can fall many times, but you won't be a failure until you say that someone else pushed you.

If you can find an excuse, don't use it. Most failures are experts at making excuses. There are always enough excuses available if you are weak enough to use them. The world simply does not have enough crutches for all the lame excuses. It's always easier to find excuses instead of time for the things we don't want to do.

The most unprofitable item ever manufactured is an excuse. So, find a way, not an excuse. There is no excuse for a human being full of excuses.

You treat others right when you don't blame them for anything that is wrong with you.

The devil eagerly waits to provide you with an excuse for every sin. An alibi is just a lie. Nothing successful is built on a falsehood.

CHAPTER 9

ONE PERSON WITH FOCUS CONSTITUTES A MAJORITY.

Focus changes everything!

The Bible says in 1 Corinthians 9:25, "To win the contest you must deny yourselves many things that would keep you from doing your best" (TLB).

Doing too many things always keeps you from doing your best.

The best way to bring focus into your life is never place a question mark where God has put a period.

Jesus warns, "No man can serve two masters: for either he will hate the one, and love the other; or else he will hold to the one, and despise the other" (Matthew 5:24).

Carl Sandberg said, "There are people who want to be everywhere at once, and they get nowhere."

God's first choice for us is not disorder, a lack of focus or waste of funds and resources.

Tim Redmond said, "Don't be a jack of all trades and a master of none. Instead be like the Apostle Paul who wrote, 'This one thing I do . . . I press towards the mark" (Philippians 3:14). What you set your heart on will determine how you will spend your life.

Few things are impossible to diligence and concentration.

Whatever you focus your attention upon, you give strength and momentum to it.

For an individual who has no focus, there is no peace.

Concentration is the secret of success.

How can you get what you want? William Locke answered, "I can tell how to get what you want; you just got to keep a thing in view and go for it, and never let your eyes wander to the right or left or up or down. And looking back is fatal."

When you serve two masters, you have to lie to one.

Ask yourself this question, "What am I really aiming at?"

George Bernard Shaw wrote, "Give a man health and a course to steer, and he will never stop to trouble about whether he is happy or not."

It's easy today to find ourselves in too much of a hurry, going too many directions, running everywhere for anything. "There is so little time for the discovery of all that we want to know about things that really interest us. We cannot afford to waste it on things that are only of casual concern for us, or in which we are interested only because other people have told us what we ought to be" (Alec Waugh).

The primary reason people fail is broken focus.

We know that Walt Disney was successful. Maybe the key to his success is found in his confession: "I love Mickey Mouse more than any women I've ever known." Now, that's focus!

Tennis legend Vic Braden said, "Losers have tons of variety. Champions take pride in just learning to hit the same old boring winners."

Consider what George Robson said after winning the Indianapolis 500: "All I had to do was keep turning left."

Do what you are doing while you are doing it.

The more complicated you are, the more ineffective you will become.

The quickest way to do many things is to do only one thing at a time.

Delegate, simplify or eliminate low priorities as soon as possible.

Do more by doing less.

I believe you will only find happiness when you are in a position of going somewhere wholeheartedly, in one direction without regret or reservation.

James Liter said, "One thought driven home is better than three left on base."

"If you chase two rabbits both will escape."

Anonymous

The only ones remembered are those who have done one thing superbly well.

Don't be like a man who said, "I'm focused, it's just on something else."

CHAPTER 10

THE WORLD BELONGS
TO THE PASSIONATE.

My friend Neil Eskelin shares this in his outstanding book, *Yes, Yes Living in a No No World,*

> "I tell about attending the awards banquet of the Chase National Life Insurance Company. The speaker was the famed author of *Think and Grow Rich,* Napoleon Hill.
>
> When Hill was introduced, it was obvious his age had caught up with him. We all wondered if the octogenarian would physically be able to give a speech. (He passed away soon after this event).
>
> Napoleon Hill slowly walked to the podium, placed both of his hands on the sides of it, looked out at the audience and announced, 'Ladies and gentlemen, I have given this speech hundreds and hundreds of times in my life. But tonight am going to deliver it the best it has ever been given. This is going to be the best speech of my life!'
>
> Wow! It was like a bolt of lightning. I watched 300 adults move to the edge of their chairs and absorb every word like a sponge."

Enthusiasm always makes others "stand up and take notice." Nothing significant is achieved without enthusiasm. Passion is the spark for your fuse.

Helen Keller said, "Optimism is the faith that leads to achievement."

Nothing will be accomplished without hope or confidence.

You can succeed at almost anything for which you have limitless zeal. Enthusiasm moves the world.

A positive attitude always creates positive results.

Your passion reflects your reserves, your unexploited resources and perhaps your future. One real difference between people is their level of passion.

Remember, some people freeze in the winter. Others ski.

Winston Churchill said, "Success is going from failure to failure without loss of enthusiasm." You will never rise to great truths and heights without joy and passion. The Bible says in 2 Chronicles 31:21, "He did it with all his heart, and prospered."

Das Energi said, "Vote with your life. Vote yes!"

"Think excitement, talk excitement, act out excitement, and you are bound to become an excited person. Life will take on a new zest, deeper interests and greater meaning. You can talk, think, and act yourself into dullness and monotony or unhappiness. By the same process you can build up inspiration, excitement and a surging depth of joy" (Norman Vincent Peale).

Attitude is a little thing that makes a big difference.

Depression, gloom, pessimism, despair, discouragement and fear slay more human beings than all illnesses combined.

You can't deliver the goods if your heart is heavier than the load.

What's enthusiasm? Henry Chester answers: "Enthusiasm is nothing more or less than faith in action."

It isn't our position but our disposition that makes us happy.

Some people count their blessings, but most think their blessings don't count.

There is a direct correlation between our passion and our potential.

The person who is negative is half-defeated before even beginning.

Enthusiasm shows God in us.

Being positive is essential to achievement and the foundation of true progress.

If you live a life of negativity, you will find yourself seasick during the entire voyage.

"We act as though comfort and luxury were the chief requirements of life, when all that we need to make us jubilant is something to be enthusiastic about."

Charles Kingsley

I agree with Winston Churchill when he said, "I am an optimist. It does not seem too much use being anything else."

Have you ever noticed that no matter how many worries a pessimist has, he always has room for one more?

Remember the Chinese proverb: "It is better to light a candle than to curse the darkness."

You can be the light of the world, but the switch must be turned on.

CHAPTER 11

TRUTH EXISTS,
LIES HAVE TO BE INVENTED.

Nine-year-old Joey was asked by his mother what he had learned in Sunday school.

"Well, Mom, our teacher told us how God sent Moses behind enemy lines on a rescue mission to lead the Israelites out of Egypt.

When he got to the Red Sea, he had his army build a pontoon bridge, and all the people walked across safely. Then, he radioed headquarters for reinforcements. They sent bombers to blow up the bridge, and all the Israelites were saved."

"Now, Joey, is that really what your teacher taught you?" his mother asked.

"Well, no, Mom. But, if I told it the way the teacher did, you'd never believe it!"

Little Joey, though well intentioned, learned you can't stretch the truth without making your story look pretty thin.

When you stretch the truth, it will snap back at you.

George Bernard Shaw said, "The liar's punishment is not in the least that he is not believed, but that he cannot believe anyone else."

There is no limit to the height a man can attain by remaining on the level.

Honesty is still the best policy. However, today there are fewer policyholders than there used to be.

George Braque said, "Truth exists; only falsehood has to be invented."

Cervantes said, "Truth will rise above falsehood as oil above water."

White lies leave black marks on a man's reputation.

Truth will win every argument if you stick with it long enough.

Though the truth may not be popular, it is always right.

The fact that nobody wants to believe something doesn't keep it from being true.

Two half-truths do not necessarily constitute the whole truth. In fact, beware of half-truths. You may have gotten hold of the wrong half.

You will find that a lie has no legs. It has to be supported by other lies.

There is no right way to do the wrong thing.

Each time you're honest you propel yourself toward greater success.

"Sin has many tools, but a lie is the handle that fits them all," said Oliver Wendell Holmes.

Those who are given to white lies soon become color blind.

You may go to the ends of the earth by lying, but you'll never get back.

Each time you lie, even with a little white lie, you push yourself toward failure.

The Bible says, "Let not mercy and truth forsake thee: bind them about thy neck; write them upon the table of thine heart" (Proverbs 3:3)

A fib starts out as a little white lie, but it usually ends up as a double feature in high definition color.

Herbert Casson said, "Show me a liar, and I will show you a thief."

The truth is one thing for which there are no known substitutes. There is no acceptable substitute for honesty. There is no valid excuse for dishonesty.

Nothing shows dirt like a white lie.

It may appear to you that a lie may take care of the present, but I want to let you know it has no future.

A shady person never produces a bright life.

An honest man changes his ideas to fit the truth, and a dishonest man alters the reality to fit his ideas.

There are no degrees of honesty.

M. Runbeck said, "There is no power on earth more formidable than the truth."

Consider what Pearl Buck said, "Truth is always exciting." Speak it, then. Life is dull without it.

CHAPTER 12

TODAY IS THE DAY TO START.

In the game of life, nothing is less important than the score at halftime.

"The tragedy of life is not that man loses, but that he almost wins."

Haywood Broun

Don't leave before the miracle happens!

Robert Louis Stevenson commented, "Saints are sinners who kept on going."

The race is not always to the swift, but to those who keep on running.

Some people wait so long the future leaves before they get there.

Today is the day to start; it's always too soon to stop.

Many times we're not to understand, just obey. The quickest way to get out of the hole is to obey God.

There's a reason God revealed the idea to you today.

"We ought to obey God rather than men."

Acts 5:29, NKJV

Choosing to follow men's ideas hinders us from hearing God's ideas.

There's a world of difference between a good idea and a God idea.

What we all need is an alarm clock that rings when it's time to rise to the occasion.

Ask yourself: "If I don't take action now, what will this ultimately cost me?"

When a procrastinator has finally made up his mind, the opportunity has already happened. Edwin Markum said,
"When duty comes a knocking at your gate,
Welcome him in; for if you bid him wait,
He will depart only to come once more
And bring seven other duties to your door."

Touch a thistle timidly, and it pricks you; grasp it boldly, and its spines crumble."

William Halsey

What you put off until tomorrow, you'll probably put off tomorrow, too.

Success comes to a man who does today what others were thinking of doing tomorrow.

Tackle any problem now—
the longer you wait, the bigger it grows.

The lazier a man is, the more he is going to do tomorrow.

All problems become smaller if you don't dodge them, but confront them.

Get aggressive and go after opportunities. They may not find you on their own.

The reason some people don't go very far in life is because they sidestep opportunity and shake hands with procrastination.

The things that come to a man who waits seldom turns out to be the things for which he's waited. The hardest task is that which was ignored yesterday.

Cervantes pondered, "By the street of By and By, one arrives at the house of never."

"Some-day" is not a day of the week.

A lazy person doesn't go through life—he's pushed through it.

"The wise man does at once what the fool does finally."

Gracian

Doing nothing is the most tiresome job in the world.

When you don't start, your difficulties won't stop.

Procrastinators never have small problems because they always wait until their problems grow up.

Procrastination is the grave in which opportunity lies.

Most people who sit around waiting for their ship to come in often find it is hardship.

Hard work is usually an accumulation of easy things never finished.

People who delay action until all factors are perfect, do nothing.

Jimmy Lyons said, "Tomorrow is the only day in the year that appeals to a lazy man."

Procrastination is the fertilizer that makes difficulties grow.

Sir Josiah Stamp said, "It is easy to dodge our responsibilities, but we cannot dodge the consequences of dodging our responsibilities."

The Bible promises no loaves to the loafer.

"A man with nothing to do does far more strenuous 'labor' than any other form of work. But my greatest pity is for the man who dodges a job he knows he should do. He is a shirker, and boy! What punishment he takes . . . from himself."

E. R. Collcord

Carve out a future; don't just whittle away the time.

The longer you take to act on God's direction, the more unclear it will become.

Be instant to obey, taking action without delay.

For the tenacious, there is always time and opportunity.

CHAPTER 13

SMALL STEPS ARE A BIG IDEA.

I remember a time in my life many years ago when I was frozen with fear at what God had called me to do. It seemed so huge a task that I was unable to bring myself to face it. A friend came to me and spoke two words that broke that paralysis in my life. He said, "Do something!" and walked out of my house. That day I "did something." Momentum came into my life, and I began to run towards the vision God had for me. Those two words were a turning point in my life.

If you are at a point of paralysis in your life because of what God wants you to do, my word for you today is "Do something!" Don't worry about the goal; just take the steps that move you past your starting point.

One thing is for sure: what isn't tried won't work.

The most important thing is to begin even though the first step is the hardest.

I agree with Vince Lombardi: "Inches make champions."

Take one small step right now.

Don't ignore the little things.

"The steps of a good man are ordered by the Lord, and He delights in his way" (Psalm 37:23, NKJV). This includes big and small steps.

Dale Carnegie said, "Don't be afraid to give your best to what seemingly are small jobs."

Every time you conquer one it makes you that much stronger.

If you do the little jobs well, the big ones will tend to take care of themselves.

Your future comes one hour at a time.

Thomas Huxley observed, "The rung of a ladder was never meant to rest upon, but to enable a man to put his other foot higher."

Other people may be smarter, better educated or more experienced than you, but no single individual has a corner on dreams, desire, or ambition.

Helen Keller said, "I long to accomplish a great and noble task, but it is my chief duty to accomplish small tasks as if they were great and noble."

The creation of a thousand forests of opportunity can spring forth from one small acorn of an idea.

My favorite prayer to pray is, "Lord, send small opportunities into my life so I can begin to use what you've put inside of me and do what you want me to do."

Never be discouraged when you make progress, no matter how slow.

Be only wary of standing still.

A success is a person who does what they can with what they have, where they are.

"Nobody makes the greater mistake than he who did nothing because he could only do a little."

Edmond Burke

All glory comes from daring to take small steps.

Small deeds done are better than great deeds planned. After being faithful in small steps, you'll look back and be able to say, "We're still not where we want to be, but we're not where we were."

Julia Carney said, "Little drops of water, little grains of sand, make the mighty ocean and the pleasant land."

Every accomplishment great or small starts with a single decision.

Even a small star shines in the darkness from millions of miles away.

Author Louis L'Amour wrote, "Victory is won not in miles but inches. Win a little now, hold your ground and later win a lot more."

God often gives us a little, in order to see what we will do with a lot.

"Though thy beginning was small, yet thy latter end should greatly increase."

Job 8:7

I believe that God cares just as much about the little things in your life as the big stuff. Why? Because He knows if you are faithful in the small things, the big things will take care of themselves.

Do little things now, and big things will come to you asking to be done.

Dante said, "From a little spark may burst a mighty flame."

Greater opportunities and joy come to those who make the most of small ones. In the parable of the talents, the master told the servant who used what he had, "Well done, good and faithful servant; you have been faithful over a few things, I will make you ruler over many things. Enter into the joy of your lord" (Matthew 25:23, NKJV).

R. Smith said, "Most of the critical things in life, which become the starting points of human destiny, are little things."

Small steps . . . what a big idea!

H. Storey remarked, "Have confidence that if you have done a little thing well, you could do a bigger thing well, too."

Value the little things. One day you may look back and realize they were large things.

CHAPTER 14

IF YOU LOOK BACK TOO MUCH, YOU'LL SOON BE HEADING THAT WAY.

Observed this conversation the other day. A young person asked a middle-aged man, "What was your favorite fast food when you were growing up?"

"We didn't have fast food when I was growing up," the man informed him. "All the food was slow."

"C'mon, seriously. Where did you eat?"

"It was a place called 'at home,'" he explained. "Mom cooked every day, and when Dad got home from work, we sat down together at the dining room table, and if I didn't like what she put on my plate I was allowed to sit there until I did like it." You should have seen the look on the kid's face. Priceless.

No one has ever backed into prosperity. You can't have a better tomorrow if you are thinking about yesterday all day today.

Believe that the best is yet to come.

Katherine Mansfield advised, "Make it a rule of life never to regret and never to look back. Regret is an appalling waste of energy. You can't build on it. It's only good for wallowing in."

I like to listen to people. I specifically like to listen to the percent of time they spend talking about the past, present and future. I've found those who predominately speak of the past are usually going backward. Those who speak of the present are just maintaining. But those who are talking about the future are growing.

Some people stay so far in the past the future is gone before they get there.

The future frightens only those who prefer living in the past.

Living in the past is an appalling waste of energy and intellect. It's like driving while looking at the rear-view mirror. The fruit of this thinking is rotten.

The past is always going to be the way it was. Stop trying to change it.

Your future contains more happiness than any past you can remember.

Consider what W. R. Ing said: "Events in the past may be roughly divided into those which probably never happened and those which do not matter."

Your past doesn't equal your future.

"Living in the past is a dull and lonely business; looking back strains the neck muscles, causing you to bump into people not going your way."

Edna Ferber

The more you look back, the less you will get ahead.

David McNally said, "Your past cannot be changed, but you can change your tomorrow by your actions today."

Thomas Jefferson was right when he said, "I like the dreams of the future better than the history of the past." Many a "has-been" lives on the reputation of his reputation.

Hubert Humphrey mused, "The good old days were never that good, believe me. The good new days are today, and better days are coming tomorrow. Our greatest songs are still unsung."

I agree with Laura Palmer's advice: "Don't waste today regretting yesterday instead of making a memory for tomorrow."

Never let yesterday use up too much of today.

Rosy thoughts about the future can't exist when your mind is full of the blues about the past.

Stop looking at where you have been and start looking at where you can be. Your destiny and call in life is always forward, never backward.

You are more likely to make mistakes when you act only on past experiences.

Phillip Raskin said, "The man who wastes today lamenting yesterday will waste tomorrow lamenting today."

Oscar Wilde said, "No man is rich enough to buy back his past."

Consider the words of the apostle Paul: "Forgetting those things which are behind and reaching forward to those things which are ahead, I press toward the goal for the prize of the upward call of God in Christ Jesus" (Philippians 3:13-14, NKJV).

Note Ecclesiastes 7:10, "Say not thou, What is the cause that the former days were better than these? for thou dost not enquire wisely concerning this."

Nothing is as far away as one hour ago.

LOOKING OUTWARD

CHAPTER 15

OBSTACLES ARE OPPORTUNITIES.

A private school in Washington faced a unique problem. A number of twelve-year-old girls were beginning to use lipstick and would put it on in the bathroom. That was fine, but after they put on their lipstick, they would press their lips to the mirror leaving dozens of little lip prints.

Every night the maintenance man would remove them, and the next day the girls would put them back.

Finally, the principal decided that something had to be done. She called all the girls to the bathroom and met them there with the maintenance man. She explained that all these lip prints were causing a major problem for the custodian who had to clean the mirrors every night (you can just imagine the yawns from the little princesses).

To demonstrate how difficult it had been to clean the mirrors, she asked the maintenance man to show the girls how much effort is required. He took out a long-handled squeegee, dipped it in the toilet, and cleaned the mirror with it.

Since then, there have been no lip prints on the mirror.

Like this example, every problem contains the seeds for its solution. You need to look for these answers creatively.

God promises a safe landing but not a calm voyage.

In the midst of challenges, God wants growth and promotion for you. Trials provide an opportunity to grow not die. Obstacles can temporarily detour you, but only you can stop. All obstacles reveal what we believe, and who we are. They introduce you to yourself.

The door to opportunity swings on the hinges of opposition.

Obstacles are opportunities for creativity. Change the way you view obstacles. They are loaded with possibilities. If you want to be a success, solve the biggest problems and discover ways to overcome the largest obstacles.

Your struggle may be lasting, but it is not everlasting.

A big lie is to think there's nothing more permanent than your temporary situation.

It's the struggle that makes you strong, because you grow through adversity not pleasure.

Oral Roberts reflects, "You cannot bring about renewal or change without confrontation."

The truth is, if you like things easy, you will have difficulties. If you like problems, you will succeed. The most successful people are those who solve the biggest problems.

When you encounter obstacles, you will discover things about yourself that you never really knew. Challenges make you stretch—they make you go beyond the norm. Martin Luther King, Jr. said, "The ultimate measure of man is not where he stands in moments of comfort and convenience, but where he stands at times of challenge and controversy."

Bob Harrison says, "Between you and anything significant will be giants in your path."

Problems are the price of progress. The obstacles of life are intended to make us better, not bitter.

Obstacles are merely a call to strengthen, not quit your resolve to achieve worthwhile goals.

Turning an obstacle to your advantage is the first necessary step towards victory. Your problem is your promotion.

Consider what Sydney Harris said, "When I hear somebody say 'Life is hard,' I am always tempted to ask, 'Compared to what?'"

Charles Kettering said, "No one would have crossed the ocean if he could have gotten off the ship in the storm."

"Times of general calamity and confusion have ever been productive of the greatest minds. The purest ore comes from the hottest furnace, and the brightest thunderbolt is the one elicited from the darkest storm."

Caleb Colton

If you have a dream without aggravations, you don't have a dream.

Have the attitude of Louisa May Alcott: "I am not afraid of storms for I am learning how to sail my ship."

Samuel Lover said, "Circumstances are the rulers of the weak, but they are the instruments of the wise."

The Chinese have this proverb that says, "The gem cannot be polished without friction, nor man perfected without trials."

It seems that great trials are a necessary preparation for greatness.

Lou Holtz advised, "Adversity is another way to measure the greatness of individuals. I never had a crisis that didn't make me stronger."

I believe every obstacle you face, God has provided a scripture for your answer.

Mike Murdock says, "If God 'cushioned' your every blow, you would never learn to grow."

Instead, don't let your problems take the lead. You take the lead.

The problem you face is simply an opportunity for you to do your best.

It is a fact; conflict is good when you know how to move with God.

What attitude do we need to have toward difficulties? William Boetcker said, "The difficulties and struggles of today are but the best price we must pay for the accomplishment and victory of tomorrow."

Life is as uncertain as a grapefruit's squirt.

The breakfast of champions is not cereal; it's obstacles.

CHAPTER 16

NO DECISION IS A DECISION.

The Bible says, "A double-minded man is unstable in all his ways." I know people who are triple- and quadruple-minded . . . I don't know what they are. It's not the difference between people that's the difficulty. It's the indifference. The fact is . . . it's a beige world. People are so lukewarm, medium, unsure, and uncommitted. All around us, fools seem to be growing without watering. So many people spend their lives failing and never even notice.

"My decision is maybe—and that's final." Is this you? Being decisive is essential for a successful life. If you deny yourself commitment, what will you do with your life? Every accomplishment, great or small, starts with a decision.

Choice, not chance, determines destiny.

You can't get a hit with the bat on your shoulder.

Nothing great happens without a decision.

Too many people go through life not knowing what they want but feeling sure they don't have it.

Herbert Prochnow said, "There is a time when we must firmly choose the course which we will follow, or the relentless drift of events will make the decision for us."

Too many people are like wheelbarrows, trailers, or canoes. They need to be pushed, pulled, or paddled.

You're either moving other people to decisions or they're moving you.

Decide to do something now to make your life better.

The choice is yours. "There's nothing in the middle of the road but yellow stripes and dead armadillos," says James Hightower.

David Ambrose remarked, "If you have the will to win, you have achieved half your success; if you don't, you have achieved half your failure."

The moment you definitely commit yourself, God moves too. All sorts of things happen to help you that never would have otherwise occurred.

"If ye will not believe, surely ye shall not be established."

Isaiah 7:9

Today, decide on your dream.

Edgar Roberts said, "Every human mind is a great slumbering power until awakened by a keen desire and a definite resolution to do."

Kenneth Blanchard observed, "There is a difference between interests and commitment. When you are interested in doing something, you only do it when it is convenient. When you are committed to something, you accept no excuses, only results."

Lack of decisiveness has caused more failures than lack of intelligence or ability.

Indecision will paralyze the flow of your faith.

Don't leave the decision for tomorrow that you should make today.

Remember, don't be a "middle-of-the-roader" because the middle of the road is the worst place to try to go forward.

Not everything that is met can be changed, but nothing can be changed until it is met.

Helen Keller said, "Science may have found a cure for most evil, but it has found no remedy for the worst of them all—the apathy of human beings."

Faith demands a decision before it can work.

"If the trumpet gives an uncertain sound, who shall prepare himself to the battle?"

1 Corinthians 14:8

You'll have the wrong foundation and won't know what to do if you're indecisive.

Maurice Witzer said, "You seldom get what you go after unless you know in advance what you want."

Indecision often gives an advantage to the other person because they did their thinking beforehand.

Every accomplishment great or small . . . starts with the decision.

Joshua encourages, "Choose for yourselves this day whom you will serve . . . ." (Joshua 24:15, NIV).

You can do everything you ought to do once you make a decision.

CHAPTER 17

COMPARISON IS NEVER PROOF.

Several years ago I met a friend whom I have known for over ten years. He looked at me and said, "John, I see all the great things that God has done in your life and how He has caused you to increase in every way. But, as I began to look at your life, I became full of doubt as to what God was doing in my life." He said, "I saw what He had done in yours, and I began to doubt that God was working in mine because I had not had the same success you have."

I turned, looked at him and said, "Well, if it's true you feel bad because God has been good to me, then would it be true that you would feel better if I had had terrible failures and had been doing much worse over the past several years?"

He gave me a quizzical look and said, "No, that would not be true."

I said, "Well if it is true for one, it is true for the other. It shows how inaccurate your thinking is. What happens in my life has nothing to do with what God is doing in your life."

Too many people know how to live everybody's life but their own.

You will find that God rarely uses people whose primary concern is what others are thinking. He loves you just as much as He loves others. Every time we put our eyes on other people, we take our eyes off the goal. I believe Jesus saw judging others as a significant waste of time. He saw that judgment halts progress. Judging others will always inhibit your forward motion.

Your faults will never vanish by calling attention to the weaknesses of others.

If you think you are doing better than the average person, you're an average person.

Why would you want to compare yourself with someone average? We need to stop comparing ourselves to others.

It isn't necessary to blow out the other person's light to let your light shine. Instead of letting their light shine, some people spend their time trying to put out the lights of others. What a waste!

"A leader is one of many accomplishments. What sets him apart from others is he is not swayed by opposition or praise or comparison," says Tim Redmond.

Pat Riley said, "Don't let other people tell you what you want."

Some are inclined to measure their achievement by what others have not done. Never measure your success by what others have or haven't done.

You are either a thermometer or a thermostat. You either register someone else's temperature or your own.

Many people have the mistaken idea that they can make themselves great by showing how small someone else is.

No one can build a personal destiny upon the faith or experience of another person.

God enters by a private door into every individual. He leads each of us by a separate path. No one can build his destiny on the success of another person. What a small man seeks is in others, what the superior man seeks is in God.

"Don't take anybody else's definition of success as your own."

Jacqueline Briskin

CHAPTER 18

THE SMALLEST DEED IS BETTER THAN THE GREATEST INTENTION.

A middle-aged man finds himself in front of the Pearly Gates. St. Peter explains that it's not so easy to get in heaven. There are some criteria before entry is allowed.

St. Peter asked, if the man was religious in life? Attend a church? The man answered, "No." St. Peter told him that's bad.

Was he generous? Give money to the poor? Charities? Again the answer was, "No." St. Peter told him that was not good.

Did he do any good deeds? Help his neighbor? Anything? Still, his answer was, "No." St. Peter was becoming concerned.

Exasperated, Peter says, "Look, everybody does something nice sometimes. Work with me, I'm trying to help. Now think!"

The man paused and said, "There was this old lady. I came out of the store and found her surrounded by a dozen Hell's Angels. They had taken her purse and were shoving her around, taunting and cursing her.

I got so mad I threw my bags down, fought through the crowd, and got her purse back. I helped her to her feet. I then went up to the biggest, baddest biker and told him how despicable, cowardly and mean he was and then spat in his face."

"Wow," said Peter, "that's impressive. When did this happen?"

"Oh, about 2 minutes ago," replied the man.

Some do things while others sit around becoming experts on how things could be done. The world divides people two ways. People who do things and people who talk about doing things. Belong to the first group—there is far less competition.

I believe the Lord didn't burden us with work. He blessed us with it. "All men are alike in their promises. It is only in their deeds that they differ" (Moliere).

Robert Half nails it: "Laziness is the secret ingredient that goes into failure, but it's only kept a secret from the person who fails."

Some people find life an empty dream because they put nothing into it.

Every time one man expresses an idea, he finds ten others who thought of it before—but took no action.

Mark Twain said, "Thunder is good, thunder is impressive, but it is lightning that does the work."

The test of this book is the reader saying not "What an inspiring book," but "I will do something!"

"Go to the ant, thou sluggard; consider her ways, and be wise: Which having no guide, overseer, or ruler, provideth her meat in the summer, and gathereth her food in the harvest" (Proverbs 6:6-8). Nothing speaks louder than this hard-working ant, yet she says nothing.

None of the secrets of success will work unless you do.

The only time a lazy person ever succeeds is when he tries to do nothing.

A famous old saying says it best: "Laziness travels so slowly; poverty soon overtakes it."

When you are lazy, you must work twice as long for half the results.

It is always a trying time for the person who is always trying to get something for nothing.

Some say nothing is impossible, yet there are a lot of people doing nothing every day.

A person who wastes enormous amounts of time talking about success will win the "prize" called failure.

What the free enterprise system means is the more enterprising you are the freer you are. What this country needs is less emphasis on free and more on enterprise.

"Striving for success without hard work is like trying to harvest where you haven't planted."

David Bly

Tell yourself: "Inspirations never go in for long engagements; they demand immediate marriage to action" (Brendon Francis).

Most of our troubles arise from loafing when we should be working and talking when we should be listening.

"There is a man in the world that never gets turned down,
wherever he chances to stray;
He gets the glad hand in the populous town,
or out where the farmers make hay;
He is greeted with pleasure on deserts of sand,
and deep in the isles of the woods;
Wherever he goes there is a welcoming hand—
he's the man who delivers the goods."

Walt Whitman

CHAPTER 19

THOSE WHO DON'T INCREASE YOU EVENTUALLY DECREASE YOU

Once upon a time, a beautiful, independent, self-assured princess happened upon a frog in a pond. The frog said to the princess, "I was once a handsome prince until an evil witch put a spell on me. One kiss from you, and I will turn back into a prince. Then we can marry and move into the castle with my mom. You can prepare my meals, clean my clothes, bear my children, and forever feel happy doing so.

Later that night, while the princess dined on frog legs, she kept laughing and saying, "I don't think so!"

If a loafer isn't a nuisance to you, it's a sign that you are somewhat of a loafer yourself.

An important attribute in successful people is their impatience with negative thinking and negative acting people.

Any time you tolerate mediocrity in others it increases your mediocrity.

You are certain to get the worst of the bargain when you exchange ideas with the wrong person.

Not everyone has a right to speak into your life.

We should not pray: "Oh Lord, deliver me from people who talk of nothing but sickness and failure." Rather "Lord, grant me the companionship of those who think success and will work for it."

Tell me who your friends are, and I will tell you who you are.

The less you associate with some people, the more your life will improve.

Almost all of our sorrows spring out of relationships with the wrong people.

"Keep out of the suction caused by those who drift backwards."

E. K. Piper

A good friend is like one mind in two bodies.

Robert Louis Stevenson said, "A friend is a present that you give yourself."

This old saying is true: "He that lies down with dogs, shall rise up with fleas."

You'll find a real true friend remains a friend even when you don't deserve to have a friend. This friend will see you through when others think that you're through.

The wisdom of Proverbs asserts, "Faithful are the wounds of a friend; but the kisses of an enemy are deceitful" (27:6).

Not everyone is for you.

I like to put it this way . . . don't follow anyone who's not going anywhere.

You and I should not follow anyone further than he or she follows Jesus Christ.

"My best friend is the man who in wishing me well wishes it for my sake."

Aristotle

The Bible declares, "As iron sharpens iron, so a man sharpens the countenance of his friend" (Proverbs 27:17, NKJV).

A true friend sees beyond you to what you can be.

Consider what Francesco Guicciardini said: "Since there is nothing so well worth having as friends, never lose a chance to make the right ones."

Thomas Carlyle observed, "Show me the man you honor, and I will know what kind of man you are, for it shows me what your ideal of manhood is, what kind of man you long to be."

The way to make a true friend is to be one.

If you were to list your most significant benefits, resources or strengths, you would find that money is one of the least important ones while some of your greatest resources are the people you know.

I believe God likes to bless people through people. He has right associations for you in your life.

Your wealth is where your friends are.

Hold a true friend with both of your hands.

CHAPTER 20

IF YOU'RE AFRAID OF CRITICISM YOU'LL DIE DOING NOTHING.

I recently spoke in front of 10,000 independent business owners. I said to them, "Tonight I am going to tell you everything I've learned from critics about how to be successful!" Then I said . . . nothing. Initially, there was complete silence in the huge arena. Then as people began to see the point I was making, applause began to break out, then more applause and shouting. Finally the whole place was cheering and clapping.

When you make your mark in life, you will always attract erasers.

To succeed in life, you must overcome the many efforts of others to pull you down.

How you choose to respond to criticism is one of the most important decisions that you make. Our response to critics should be what the Bible says, "We are perplexed, but not in despair; persecuted, but not forsaken; cast down, but not destroyed."

One of the easiest things to find is fault.

Love your enemies, but if you want to make them mad, ignore them completely.

It is the still small voice we should heed; not the deafening blasts of doom.

If your head sticks up above the crowd, expect more criticism than bouquets.

Weak people always attack those who are moving forward.

God works from the inside out; a critic tries to work from the outside in.

The first and great commandment about critics is: Don't let them scare you.

Charles Dodgson said, "If you limit your actions in life to things that nobody could possibly find fault with, you will not do much."

Nothing significant happens without controversy, without criticism.

Christopher Morley said, "The truth is, a critic is like a gong at a railroad crossing, clanging loudly and vainly as the train goes by."

Many great ideas die because people who had them couldn't stand the criticism and gave up.

A critic is simply someone who finds fault without a search warrant.

When you allow other people's words to stop you, they will.

Critics aren't interested in making things better. They want to pull you down to their level. They are afraid you might succeed.

I agree with Fred Allen, "If criticism had any real power to harm, the skunk would have been extinct by now."

Great minds discuss ideas, good minds discuss events, and small minds discuss other people.

Don't allow yourself to become a critic. Jesus warns, "Judge not, that ye be not judged" (Matthew 7:1).

The mud thrower never has clean hands.

You will never move up if you are continually running someone down.

I agree with Tillotson: "There is no readier way for a man to bring his worth into question than by endeavoring to detract from the worth of other men."

If you are afraid of criticism, you will die with little or nothing.

Dennis Wholey warned, "Expecting the world to treat you fairly because you are a good person is a little like expecting a bull not to attack you because you are a vegetarian."

You can't carve your way to success with cutting remarks.

Criticism is a compliment when you know what you're doing is right.

CHAPTER 21

IF YOU ARE ONLY LOOKING OUT FOR YOURSELF, LOOK OUT!

Wesley Huber said, "There is nothing quite so dead as a self-centered man—a man who holds himself up as a self-made success, and measures himself by himself and is pleased with the result."

Is your favorite letter "I"?

Listen: "The core of sin is 'I' no matter how you spell it" (Ed Cole).

The only reason pride lifts you up is to let you down.

What means most in life is what you've done for others.

The best way to encourage yourself is to try to encourage somebody else.

It's the duty of all leaders to make it difficult for others to do wrong, easy to do right.

Egotism blossoms but bears no fruit.

"Those who bring sunshine to the lives of others cannot keep it from themselves."

James Matthew Barrie

Leave people better than you found them. After people have been around you, do they feel better or worse? Bigger or smaller? More full of faith or fear? Are you leaving people better than you found them?

Norman Vincent Peale observed, "The man who lives for himself is a failure. Even if he gains much wealth, power or position he is still a failure."

Conceit makes us fools: "Do you see a man wise in his own eyes? There is more hope for a fool than for him" (Proverbs 26:12, NIV).

Those who sing their own praises seldom receive an encore.

Charles Elliot intones, "Don't think too much of yourself. Try to cultivate the habit of thinking of others; this will reward you. Selfishness always brings its own revenge."

An egotist is his own best friend.

The best way to be happy is to forget yourself and focus on other people.

Henry Courtney said, "The bigger a man's head gets, the easier it is to fill his shoes."

Even postage stamps become useless when they get stuck on themselves.

The man who believes in nothing but himself lives in a tiny world.

Egotism is the only disease where the patient feels well while making everyone else around him feel sick.

While gazing upon selfish accomplishments, the arrogant often miss God by failing to see what He is doing.

Rick Renner said, "Don't miss the plan of God by self-consumption."

When you are on a high horse, the best thing to do is to dismount at once.

You can't push yourself forward by patting yourself on the back.

A swelled head always proves there is plenty of room for improvement.

Burton Hillis remarked, "It's fine to believe in ourselves, but we mustn't be too easily convinced."

The fellow who is deeply in love with himself should get a divorce.

"The greatest magnifying glasses in the world are a man's own eyes when they look upon his own person."

Alexander Pope

Folks who boast of being self-made usually have a few parts missing.

You can recognize a self-made man; his head is oversized, and he has arms long enough to pat himself on the back.

A conceited person never gets anywhere because he thinks he is already there.

CHAPTER 22

ENVY IS EMPTY.

People who are envious always are quick to find the negative. There was a hunter who came into the possession of a special bird dog. The dog was the only one of its kind, because it can walk on water. One day he invited a friend to go hunting with him so that he could show off his prized possession.

After some time, they shot a few ducks, which fell into the river. The man ordered his dog to run and fetch the birds. The dog ran on top of the water to collect the birds. The man was expecting a compliment about the amazing dog but did not receive it.

Being curious, he asked his friend if he had noticed anything unusual about the dog. The friend replied, "Yes, I did see something unusual about your dog. Your dog can't swim!"

Most of the people we face every day are negative. They choose to look at the hole in the middle rather than the donut. Do not expect compliments or encouragement from them. These are the people who cannot pull you out of your present situation. They can only push you down.

If envy were a disease, everyone would be sick.

Frances Bacon said, "Envy has no holidays. It has no rest."

Envy is a ridiculous idea. It offers no single advantage. A famous old saying said, "When you compare what you want with what you have, you will be unhappy. Instead, compare what you deserve with what you have, and you'll discover happiness." It's not trying to keep up with the Joneses that causes so much trouble. It's speeding to pass them. Washington Allston reflected, "The only competition worthy of a wise mind is within himself." Nothing gets you behind faster than trying to keep up with people who are already there.

"But they are only comparing themselves with each other, and measuring themselves by themselves. What foolishness!" (2 Corinthians 10:12b, NLT)

Thomas Fuller said, "Comparison, more than reality, makes men happy or wretched."

St. Chrysostom reflected, "As a moth gnaws a garment, so doeth envy consume a man."

Envy provides the mud that failure throws at success.

What makes us discontented with our personal condition is the absurd belief that others are so much happier that we are.

You'll find it's hard to be happier than others if you believe others to be happier than they are.

Envy consumes nothing but its own heart.

One of the most valuable decisions we can make is to not be influenced in our lives by what's happening in other people's lives. What occurs in someone else's life has nothing to do with what God wants to do in yours. He loves you just as much as He loves others. Every time we put our eyes on other people, we take our eyes off the goal.

There are many roads to an unsuccessful life, but envy is the shortest of them all.

Envy is one of the subtlest forms of judging others.

Richard Evans said, "May we never let the things we can't have or don't have, spoil our enjoyment of the things we do have and can have."

Worry about what other people think of you, and you'll have more confidence in their opinion than you have in your own.

CHAPTER 23

TRAVEL LIGHT.

Don't let things stick to you.

It is far better to forgive and forget than to hate and remember.

Josh Billings says, "There is no revenge so complete as forgiveness."

Richard Nixon said, "Those who hate you don't win unless you hate them, and then you destroy yourself."

Unforgiveness blocks blessings; forgiveness releases blessings.

Why aren't some prayers answered? Dwight L. Moody replied, "I firmly believe that a great many prayers are not answered because we are not willing to forgive someone."

Forgiveness is the key to personal peace.

Forgiveness releases action and creates freedom.

Forgiveness saves the expense of anger, the high cost of hatred, and a terrible waste of energy.

Forgiveness heals; unforgiveness wounds.

Be quick to forgive. I believe that the longer we take to forgive, the harder it is to do. People need loving the most when they deserve it the least. Matthew 5:25 says, "Come to terms quickly with your enemy before it is too late" (NLT). The best healing is a quick healing.

It's true . . . the one who forgives ends the quarrel.

Do you want to release the past and claim the future? Get a hold of what Paul Boese said: "Forgiveness does not change the past, but it does enlarge the future."

Patting a person on the back is the best way to get a chip off his shoulder.

Forgive your enemies—you can't get back at them any other way!

Is there anything more pathetic than a person who's harbored a grudge for many years!

"Protest long enough that you are right and you will be wrong."

Yiddish proverb

We all need to say the right thing after doing the wrong thing.

Lawrence Sterne said, "Only the brave know how to forgive . . . a coward never forgave; it is not in his nature."

Josiah Bailey adds, "It is the truth that those who forgive most shall be most forgiven."

One of the secrets of a long and fruitful life is to forgive everybody everything every night before you go to bed.

Peter Von Winter said, "It is manlike to punish, but Godlike to forgive."

When you have a huge chip on your shoulder, it causes you to lose your balance.

Travel light. The heaviest thing a person can carry is a grudge. If you stop nursing it, it will die. You don't need a doctor to tell you it's better to remove a grudge than to nurse it.

You can be wrong in the middle of being right when you don't forgive someone.

Ask yourself this question, "If God is willing to forgive, then who am I to hold out?"

Forgiveness is a funny thing. It warms the heart and cools the sting.

The Bible says in Ephesians, "Let all bitterness, and wrath, and anger, and clamour, and evil speaking, be put away from you, with all malice: And be ye kind one to another, tenderhearted, forgiving one another, even as God for Christ's sake hath forgiven you" (4:31).

Harry Fosdick said, "No one can be wrong with man and right with God."

CHAPTER 24

IF YOU HAVE, GIVE.
IF YOU LACK, GIVE.

G. D. Bordmen said, "The law of the harvest is to reap more than you sow." It is true: people who give, always receive. What you give lives. Henry Drummond said, "There is no happiness in having or in getting, but only in giving." The test of generosity is not necessarily how much you give but how much you have left. Henry Thoreau said, "If you give money, spend yourself with it." The secret to living is giving.

Charles Spurgeon said, "Feel for others—in your wallet."

An Indian proverb says, "Good people, like clouds, receive only to give away."

In fact, the best generosity is that which is quick. When you give quickly, it is like giving twice.

Greed diminishes whatever's gained. Mike Murdock says, "Giving is proof that you have conquered greed."

A lot of people are willing to give God the credit, but not too many are willing to give Him the cash.

A mother was preparing pancakes for her sons, Kevin, age five, and Ryan, age three. The boys began to argue over who would get the first pancake.

Their mother saw the opportunity for a moral lesson. "If Jesus were sitting here, He would say, 'Let my brother have the first pancake, I can wait.'"

Kevin turned to his younger brother and said, "Ryan, you be Jesus!"

Don't wait on other people to be generous.

Give quickly. The longer you take to give the less likely you are to do it. You grow spiritually to the extent you give out. By giving out, you create room to grow on the inside. Be generous no matter your current circumstances.

Christine Caine says, "Time, talent, tongue and treasure are what you have to give. Don't be deterred by what you don't have. If you do, you'll miss what you do have. Stop saying, "I've only got___.""

A good way to judge a man is by what he says. A better way is by what he does. The best way is by what he gives.

The big problem is not the haves and have nots—it's the give nots. The Lord loves a cheerful giver, and so does everyone else.

R. Browne says, "Whatever God does in your life is not so you can keep it to yourself. He wants you to give to others."

Elizabeth Bibesco said, "Blessed are those who can give without remembering and take without forgetting."

When you give only after being asked, you have waited too long.

Give thanks for your daily bread.
Give your best time to communion with God.
Give out of your first fruits.
Give quickly.
Give back.
Give until it feels good.
Give sincere compliments.
Give thanks to God.

The Bible says in Acts, "It is more blessed to give than to receive" (20:35, NIV).

The Swiss say, "A greedy person and a pauper are practically one in the same."

Eleanor Roosevelt said, "When you cease to make a contribution, you begin to die."

Getters don't get happiness. Givers get it.

When you live for another, it's the best way to live for yourself.

Giving is always the thermometer of our love.

John Wesley advised, "Make all you can, save all you can, give all you can." That's a right formula for a successful life.

When it comes to giving, some people stop at nothing.

Don't cheat the Lord and call it savings.

The trouble with too many people who give until it hurts is that they are so sensitive to pain.

CHAPTER 25

THE BEST OPPORTUNITY IS NOW.

The boss wondered why one of his most dependable and valued employees had phoned in sick one day. Having an urgent problem with one of the main computers, he dialed the employee's home phone number and was greeted with a child's whisper.

"Hello?"

"Is your daddy home?" he asked.

"Yes," whispered the small voice.

"May I talk with him?"

The child whispered, "No."

Surprised and still wanting to talk with an adult, the boss asked, "Is your mommy there?"

"Yes."

"May I talk with her?"

Again the small voice whispered, "No."

Hoping there was somebody with whom he could leave a message, the boss asked, "Is anybody else there?"

"Yes," whispered the child, "a policeman."

Wondering what a cop would be doing at his employee's home, the boss asked, "May I speak with the policeman?"

"No, he's busy," whispered the child.

"Busy doing what?"

"Talking to Mummy and Daddy," came the whispered answer.

Growing more worried as he heard a loud noise in the background through the earpiece on the phone, the boss asked, "What is that noise?"

"A helicopter," answered the whispering voice.

"What is going on there?" demanded the boss, now truly apprehensive.

Again, whispering, the child answered, "The search team just landed a helicopter."

Alarmed, concerned and a little frustrated the boss asked, "What are they searching for?"

Still whispering, the young voice replied with a muffled giggle . . . "Me."

Horatio Dresser said, "The ideal never comes. Today is ideal for him who makes it so."

What you're looking for is many times right under your nose.

Live for today. Don't let what you have within your grasp today be missed entirely because only the future intrigued you and the past disheartened you.

Wayne Dyer observed, "Now is all we have. Everything that has ever happened, anything that is ever going to happen to you, is just a thought."

Marie Edgeworth said, "There is no moment like the present. The man who will not execute his resolutions when they are fresh on him can have no hope from them afterwards; for they will be dissipated, lost, and perished in the hurry and scurry of the world, or sunk in the slough of indolence."

Today was once the future from which you expected so much in the past.

The Bible says, "So, teach us to number our days, that we may apply our hearts unto wisdom" (Psalm 90:12).

What you want is close to you. Know the real value of today. I agree with Jonathan Swift when he said, "May you live all the days of your life." The future that you long and dream for begins today.

Ralph Waldo Emerson said, "Write it on your heart that every day is the best day of the year."

There are seeds of success in your hand right now.

The regrets that most people experience in life come from failing to act when having an opportunity.

Heed 2 Corinthians 6:2: "Now is the accepted time."

"Miracles are coming by you or to you every day."

Oral Roberts

The most important thing in our lives is what we are doing now.

I agree with Martial when he said, "Tomorrow life is too late; live today."

Today, well lived, will prepare you for both the opportunities and obstacles of tomorrow.

Be thankful for what you have and where you are.

God always starts with what you have where you are to take you to where He wants you to be.

Don't be caught out in the backyard looking for four-leaf clovers when opportunity knocks at your front door.

Many spend too much time dreaming of the future, never realizing that a little of it arrives every day.

Seneca said, "Begin at once to live."

Ellen Metcalf remarked, "There are many people who are at the right place at the right time but don't know it."

John Burroughs said, "The lesson which life repeats and constantly reinforces is, 'Look under foot.' You are always nearer than you think . . . . The great opportunity is where you are. Do not despise your place and hour."

Seize the moment!

It is okay to take time to plan, but when the time for action has arrived, stop thinking and go for it!

Albert Dunning said, "Great opportunities come to all, but many do not know that they have met them. The only preparation to take advantage of them is . . . to watch what each day brings."

Doing the best at this moment puts you in the best place for the next moment. When can you live if not now? All the flowers of tomorrow are in the seeds of today.

Few know when to rise to the occasion. Most only know when to sit down.

I agree with Ruth Schabacker when she said, "Every day comes bearing its own gifts. Untie the ribbons."

CHAPTER 26

A GOOD WAY TO FORGET YOUR TROUBLES IS TO HELP OTHERS OUT OF THEIRS.

Leave people better than you found them whether they appreciate it or not. After people have been around you, do they feel better or worse? Bigger or smaller? More full of faith or fear? Are you leaving people better than you found them?

A beautiful thing a person can do for his Heavenly Father is to be kind to His children.

Serving others is one of this life's most awesome privileges.

Albert Schweitzer said, "The only ones among you who will really be happy are those who have sought and found how to serve."

Hunt for the good points in people. Remember they have to do the same in your case. Then do something to help them.

I agree with Henry Drummond when he said, "I wonder why it is that we are not kinder to each other . . . how much the world needs it! How easily it is done!"

Follow the counsel of Carl Reilland: "In about the same degree as you are helpful, you will be happy."

Pierre de Chartin commented, "The most satisfying thing in life is to have been able to give a large part of oneself to others." Proverbs declares, "He who despises his neighbor sins; but he who has mercy on the poor, happy is he" (14:21, NKJV).

"What we do for ourselves alone dies with us; what we do for others lives beyond us. What I gave, I have, what I spent, I had, what I kept, I lost."

Old epitaph

No man is more deceived than the selfish man.

"No man was ever honored for what he received. Honor has been the reward for what he gave," said Calvin Coolidge.

"The Golden Rule is of no use unless we realize it's our turn."

Dr. Frank Crane

Invest in the success of others. When you help someone up a mountain, you'll find yourself close to the summit, too.

If you want to get ahead, be a bridge not a wall.

Love others more than they deserve.

Each human being presents us with an opportunity to serve.

Everybody needs help from everybody.

What means most in life is what you've done for others.

The best way to encourage yourself is to try to encourage somebody else.

It's the duty of all leaders to make it difficult for others to do wrong, easy to do right.

John Andrew Holmes said, "The entire population of the universe, with one trifling exception, is composed of others."

Kindness is one of the most difficult things to give away since it usually comes back to you.

The person who sows seeds of kindness enjoys a perpetual harvest.

Too often we expect everyone else to practice the golden rule.

The golden rule may be old, but it isn't used enough to show any signs of wear.

We make a first-class mistake if we treat others as a second-class people.

You can't help others without helping yourself.

Do you want to get along better with others? Be a little kinder than necessary.

A good way to forget your troubles is to help others out of theirs.

"Those who bring sunshine to the lives of others cannot keep it from themselves."

James Matthew Barrie

When you share, you do not lessen, but increase your life.

Theodore Spear said, "You can never expect too much of yourself in the matter of giving yourself to others."

The taller the bamboo grows, the lower it bends.

Harry Fosdick said, "One of the most amazing things ever said on earth is Jesus' statement, 'He that is greatest among you shall be your servant.' No one will be thought of as significant a century after they're gone, except those who have been servants of all."

Martin Luther King, Jr. said, "Everybody can be great . . . because anybody can serve."

When you walk in the fruit of the Spirit, others can taste of it.

"Have you had a kindness shown?
Pass it on!
'Twas not given for thee alone,
Pass it on!
Let it travel down the years,
Let it wipe another's tears,
Till in heaven the deed appears
Pass it on!"

Henry Burton

CHAPTER 27

YOU CAN LEARN SOMETHING FROM EVERYONE.

A teacher told her young class to ask their parents for a family story with a moral at the end of it, and to return the next day to tell their stories.

In the classroom the next day, Joe gave his example first, "My dad is a farmer and we have chickens. One day we were taking lots of eggs to market in a basket on the front seat of the truck when we hit a big bump in the road; the basket fell off the seat and all the eggs broke. The moral of the story is not to put all your eggs in one basket."

"Very good," said the teacher.

Next, Mary said, "We are farmers too. We had twenty eggs waiting to hatch, but when they did we only got ten chicks. The moral of this story is not to count your chickens before they're hatched."

"Very good," said the teacher again, very pleased with the response so far.

Next it was Barney's turn to tell his story: "My dad told me this story about my Aunt Karen. . . . Aunt Karen was a flight engineer in the war, and her plane got hit. She had to bail out over enemy territory, and all she had was a bottle of whiskey, a machine gun and a machete."

"Go on," said the teacher, intrigued.

"Aunt Karen drank the whiskey on the way down to prepare herself; then she landed right in the middle of a hundred enemy soldiers. She killed seventy of them with the machine gun until she ran out of bullets. Then she killed twenty more with the machete till the blade broke. And then she killed the last ten with her bare hands."

"Good heavens," said the horrified teacher. "What did your father say was the moral of that frightening story?"

"Stay away from Aunt Karen when she's been drinking . . . " You can learn something from everyone and everything.

The biggest room in our house is always the room for self-improvement.

Goethe said, "Everybody wants to be; nobody wants to grow."

Have you ever noticed there are people you know who are literally at the same place today as they were five years ago? They still have the same dreams, the same problems, the same alibis, the same opportunities and the same way of thinking. They are standing still in life.

Many people unplug their clocks at a particular point in time and stay at that fixed moment the rest of their lives. God's will for us is to grow, to continue to learn and improve.

It's true, today a reader, tomorrow a leader.

A famous saying reads: "It's what you learn after you know it all that counts." I must admit that I am somewhat of a fanatic about this. I hate to have idle time—time in which I am not learning anything. Those around me know that I must always have something to read or to write during any idle moment that might arise. In fact, I try to learn from everyone. From one, I may learn what not to do, while from another, I learn what to do. Learn from the mistakes of others. You can never live long enough to make all the mistakes yourself.

I agree with Van Crouch: "You will never change your actions until you change your mind." An important way to keep increasing is never to stop asking questions.

You can learn more from a wise man when he is wrong than a fool who is right.

I've known countless people who were excellent reservoirs of learning yet never had an outstanding idea. "Eyes that look are common. Eyes that see are rare," says J. Oswald Sanders. The problem is we're flooded with information and starving for revelation.

You can't see the sunrise by looking to the west.

We should all know what we are running from and to and why.

To resist or receive is a decision we make every day.

It's fun to keep learning.

Nothing dies quicker than a new idea in a closed mind.

The person who is afraid of asking is ashamed of learning.

Only hungry minds can grow.

We should learn as if we will live forever and live as if we are going to die tomorrow.

Harvey Ullman said, "Anyone who stops learning is old, whether this happens at 20 or 80. Anyone who keeps on learning not only remains young but becomes consistently more valuable regardless of physical capacity."

Learning brings promotion to your life.

Learn from others. Learn to see in the challenges of others, the pitfalls you should avoid.

Experience is a present instructor who keeps us from repeating the past in the future.

Life teaches us by giving us new problems before we solve the old ones.

"It is impossible for a man to learn what he thinks he already knows."

Epictetus

Timothy instructed: "Study to shew thyself approved unto God . . . ." (2 Timothy 2:15).

Think education is expensive or difficult? Listen to Derek Bok: "If you think education is expensive—try ignorance."

CHAPTER 28

IGNORE WHAT PEOPLE SAY CAN'T BE DONE.

I love what LifeChurch.tv has as a core value for its church. "We are faith-filled, big-thinking, bet-the-farm risk takers. We'll never insult God with small thinking and safe living." This core value is one we all should have.

Until you give yourself to some great cause, you haven't begun to live fully.

Grandmother saw Billy running around the house slapping himself and asked him why. "Well," said Billy, "I just got so tired of walking I thought I'd ride my horse for a while."

A genius is someone who shoots at something no one else sees and hits it.

Nothing significant is ever accomplished by a realistic person.

Tradition offers no hope for the present and makes no preparation for the future.

Be like David. Find a giant and slay it.

"We are told never to cross a bridge till we come to it, but this world is owned by men who have 'crossed bridges' in their imagination far ahead of the crowd."

Speakers Library

Our challenge is to observe the future and act before it occurs.

We should do that which takes us out of our comfort zone.

Always pick an obstacle big enough to matter when you overcome it.

Dream big because we serve a big God.

One day Michelangelo saw a block of marble, which the owner said, was of no value. "It is valuable to me," said Michelangelo. "There is an angel imprisoned in it and I must set it free."

Many times we act, or fail to act, not because of "will," as is so commonly believed, but because of imagination.

Henry Miller commented, "The man who looks for security, even in the mind, is like a man who would chop off his limbs in order to have artificial ones which would never give him pain or trouble."

Melvin Evans said, "The men who build the future are those who know that greater things are yet to come and that they will help bring them about. Their minds expand from the blazing sun of hope. They never stop to doubt. They haven't time."

Day by day, year by year, broaden your horizon.

Russell Davenport remarked, "Progress in every age results only from the fact that there are some men and women who refuse to believe that what they knew to be right cannot be done."

Know the rules and then break some of them.

Be a mind through which Christ thinks; a heart through which Christ loves; a voice through which Christ speaks; and a hand with which Christ helps.

Take the lid off.

Your dreams are an indicator of your potential greatness, and you'll know it's God-given because it comes to you with the force of a revelation.

Do a right-about-face that turns you from failure to success. Keep this formula in mind: always act as if it's impossible to fail.

Be involved in something bigger than you. God has never had anyone qualified to work for Him yet. "We are the wire, God is the current. Our only power is to let the current pass through it" (Carlo Carretto).

If you want to defend what you believe, live it.

Dorothea Brand stated, "All that is necessary to break the spell of inertia and frustration is this: act as if it were impossible to fail."

One of the greatest pleasures you can find is doing what people say you cannot do.

LOOKING UPWARD

CHAPTER 29

DON'T JUST LOOK FOR MIRACLES YOU ARE A MIRACLE.

"My mother said to me, 'If you become a soldier you'll become a general, if you become a monk you end up as the pope.' Instead, I became a painter and wound up as Picasso," said the great painter. No one ever became great by imitation. Don't be a copy of something. Make your own impression.

An original is hard to find but easy to recognize.

"If God had wanted you otherwise, He would have created you otherwise."

Goethe

Dare to be what you are. Resolve to be yourself.

A Congolese proverb asserts, "Wood may remain ten years in the water, but it will never become a crocodile."

The Bible asks, "Can the Ethiopian change his skin or the leopard its spots?" (Jeremiah 13:23, NIV)

Never wish to be anything but what you are.

Julius Hare advises, "Be what you are. This is the first step towards becoming better than you are."

The person who trims himself to suit everybody will soon whittle himself away.

All people are created equal and endowed by their Creator with a mighty urge to become otherwise.

If you don't have a plan for your life, you'll only become a part of someone else's.

You can't carry two faces under one hat.

"It is better to be hated for what you are, than loved for what you are not."

Andre Gide

"All the discontented people I know are trying to be something they are not, to do something they cannot do."

David Grayson

When you use the gifts you have, people call you gifted.

One of the hardest things about climbing the ladder of success is getting through the crowd of copies at the bottom. How many outstanding generalities do you know?

When you do not dare to be yourself, you will lack confidence and will crave admiration continually. You will live on the reflection of yourself in the eyes of others.

"The curious paradox is that when I accept myself just as I am, then I can change."

Carl Rogers

Don't try and live up to anyone's expectations but God's.

Worn out paths are for worn out men.

Friedrich Klopstock remarked, "He who has no opinion of his own, but depends on the opinions of others is a slave. To only dream of the person you are supposed to be is to waste the person you are."

Nobody is so disappointed and so unhappy as a person who longs all of life to be somebody other than who he really is.

You are "fearfully and wonderfully made" (Psalm 139:14, NIV).

The copy adapts himself to the world, but an original tries to adapt the world to him. Therefore, all progress depends upon originals.

Doris Mortman observed, "Until you make peace with who you are, you will never be content with what you have."

Don't be awestruck by other people and try to copy them.

Nobody can be you as efficiently and as effectively as you can.

"Don't copy the behaviors and customs of this world, but be a new and different person with a fresh newness in all you do and think. Then you will learn from your own experience how his ways will really satisfy you" (Romans 12:2, TLB).

"Man is more interesting than men. It's him, not them, whom God made in his image. Each is more precious than all."

Andre Gide

"All good things which exist are the fruit of originality."

John Mills

There is only one life for each of us—our own.

The person who walks in another's tracks never leaves his own footprints.

Leo Buscaglia counseled, "The easiest thing to be in the world is you. The most difficult thing to be is what other people want you to be. Don't let them put you in that position."

Most of our challenges in life come from not knowing ourselves and ignoring our best, real virtues.

Most people live their entire lives as complete strangers to themselves. Don't let that happen to you.

Imitation is limitation.

The Bible says in 1 Kings, "Why are you pretending to be someone else?" (14:6, NLT)

The opposite of courage is not fear. It is conformity.

The most exhausting and frustrating thing in life is to live it trying to be someone else.

CHAPTER 30

CALL HOME. YOUR HEAVENLY FATHER WANTS TO TALK TO YOU.

"The best prayers have often more groans than words" (John Bunyan). I experienced this when I had many pressing needs all around me. Honestly, I reached a point where I could hardly pray about my needs because they were so many. The only prayer I could manage was, "Help!" and I remember passionately praying it to God over 30 times until I experienced a breakthrough. Psalms declares, "O Lord, attend to my cry" (17:1, NKJV). One of the smartest things I ever prayed was, "Help!" When you take one step toward God, God will take more steps toward you than you could ever count. He moved to meet my needs.

The sweetest lesson I have learned in God's school is to let the Lord choose for me."

Do deep praying before you find yourself in a deep hole.

Prayers are only answered after they are prayed.

Nothing significant happens until you fervently pray; pray until you pray!

A pastor asked a little boy if he said his prayers every night.

"Yes sir," the boy replied.

"And, do you always say them in the morning, too?" the pastor asked.

"No sir," the boy replied. "I ain't scared in the daytime."

Any time is a good time to talk to the Lord. Good times and bad. Happy or sad. Smiling or scared. He loves to hear from you and me.

Prayer alone proves that you trust God.

Unfortunately, nothing is discussed more and practiced less than prayer.

Oswald Chambers said, "We look upon prayer as a means of getting things for ourselves; the Bible idea of prayer is that we may get to know God Himself." Follow Dwight L. Moody's advice: "Spread out your petition before God and then say, 'Thy will, not mine, be done.'"

"Every time we pray our horizon is altered, our attitude to change is altered, not sometimes but every time. The amazing thing is that we don't pray more."

Oswald Chambers

Margaret Gibb said, "We must move from asking God to take care of the things that are breaking our hearts, to praying about the things that are breaking His heart."

Amazing things start happening when we start praying. Prayer time is never wasted time. Charles Spurgeon taught, "Sometimes we think we are too busy to pray. That is a great mistake, for praying is a savings of time."

A. J. Gordon added, "You can do more than pray after you have prayed, but you cannot do more than pray until you have prayed."

Pray with your eyes toward God, not toward your problems.

Byron Edwards said, "True prayer always receives what it asks for—or something better."

God's answers are wiser than your answers.

Ann Lewis said, "There are four ways God responds to prayer: no, not yet; no, I love you too much; yes, I thought you'd never ask; yes, and here's more."

It is impossible to be prayerful and pessimistic at the same time.

E. M. Bounds said, "Prayer is our most formidable weapon; the thing which makes all else we do efficient."

Prayer is not a gadget we use when nothing else works. Rather, I agree with O. Hallesby when he said, "Begin to realize more and more that prayer is the most important thing you do. You can use your time to no better advantage than to pray whenever you have an opportunity to do so, either alone or with others; while at work, while at rest, or while walking down the street. Anywhere!"

Mark Litteton said, "Turn your doubts to questions; turn your questions to prayers; turn your prayers to God."

Frequent kneeling will keep you in good standing with God.

Martin Luther said, "The less I pray, the harder it gets; the more I pray the better it goes."

When praying, we must simultaneously be willing to take the action God directs in the answer to our prayer. The answers to your prayers will include work. Action is attached to answers and success.

When you pray for victory, God will give you a strategy.

Phillips Brooks said, "Prayer is not conquering God's reluctance but taking hold of God's willingness."

CHAPTER 31

EXCEEDING ABUNDANTLY ABOVE ALL THAT WE ASK OR THINK

When I wrote my first book, *An Enemy Called Average*, in 1990, I decided from the start to sign every book with the phrase "Launch Out." Well, I had no idea how that simple phrase would resonate with my readers. I had people quit their jobs, change careers and go in directions they never thought they could. Jesus was my original source for this expression when He said to His disciple Simon, "Launch out into the deep for a catch of fish." He knew they needed to go further, deeper to get the result they desired. So do we.

"For many years 'Safety first' has been the motto of the human race . . . but it has never been the motto of leaders. A leader must face danger. He must take the risk and the blame and the brunt of the storm."

Herbert Casson

If you want to be successful, leave your comfort zone. Step out by faith to the place where if God is not in it, it won't succeed.

Elizabeth Kenny reflected, "It is better to be a lion for a day than a sheep all your life."

Everybody dies, but not everyone has lived.

You can't get your head above water if you never stick your neck out.

A dream that does not include a risk is not worthy of being called a dream.

Halifax said, "The man who leaves nothing to chance will do few things badly, but he will do very few things."

If you never take risks, you'll never accomplish great things.

Recently, I saw a plaque that said, "Excellence can be attained if you . . . Care more than others think is wise, Risk more than others think is safe, Dream more than others think is practical, Expect more than others think is possible."

C. S. Lewis said, "The safest road to hell is a gradual one—the gentle slope, soft underfoot, without sudden turnings, without milestones, without signposts."

Unless a man takes on more than he possibly can do, he will never do all he can.

If you dare for nothing, you need hope for nothing.

The readiness to take risks is our grasp of faith.

"Don't be afraid to take a big step if one is indicated; you can't cross a chasm in two small jumps," said William Lloyd George.

Your vision must be larger than you.

We should say "Lead me to the rock that is higher than I." (Psalm 61:2, NKJV).

"Don't avoid extremes to stay 'in balance,' stay in balance by living in the extreme God wills at that time in your life."

Tim Redmond

"Brethren, be great believers. Little faith will bring your souls to heaven, but great faith will bring heaven to your souls," said Charles Spurgeon.

Whenever you see a successful person, I guarantee that person took risks and made courageous decisions. Success favors the bold. The world is a book where those who do not take risks read only one page. David Mahoney said, "Refuse to join the cautious crowd that plays not to lose. Play to win."

You have a chance to improve yourself. Just believe in taking chances.

If you don't risk anything, you risk even more.

Chuck Yeager remarked, "You don't concentrate on risk. You focus on results. No risk is too great to prevent the necessary job from getting done."

John Newman wrote, "Calculation never made a hero."

Every person has a chance to improve himself, but some just don't believe in taking chances.

You'll always miss 100% of the shots that you don't take.

Stemmons said, "When your chances are slim and none . . . go with slim."

Morris West said, "If you spend your whole life inside waiting for the storms, you'll never enjoy the sunshine."

Listen to Conrad Hilton: "I encourage boldness because the danger of seniority and pension plans tempt a young man to settle in a rut named security rather than find his own rainbow."

No one reaches the top without daring.

Metastaisio observed, "Every noble acquisition is attended with its risk; he who fears to encounter the one must not expect to obtain the other."

If you have found yourself throughout life never scared, embarrassed, disappointed or hurt it means you have never taken any chances.

I agree with Lois Platford when she said, "You have all eternity to be cautious and then you're dead." Being destined for greatness requires you to take risks and confront significant hazards.

Listen to Tommy Barnett: "Many people believe that you are really walking by faith when there is no risk but the truth is the longer you walk with God . . . the greater the risk."

David Viscot wrote, "If your life is ever going to get better, you'll have to take risks. There is simply no way you can grow without taking chances."

CHAPTER 32

DO YOU COUNT YOUR BLESSINGS OR THINK YOUR BLESSINGS DON'T COUNT?

I remember several years ago driving to dinner, completely absorbed in thought about my latest book. So focused that I drove right through a red light at a major intersection.

After being greeted by several horns and one man who wanted to let me know with his finger that "I was number one," I pulled into the parking lot to give thanks to God for His protection, even when I'm stupid.

Know that you are blessed. Know that you are blessed.

"If the only prayer you say in your whole life is 'Thank you,' that would suffice."

Miester Eckhart

Do you have an attitude of gratitude?

If we stop to think more, we will stop to thank more.

Erich Fromm remarked, "Greed is a bottomless pit which exhausts the person in an endless effort to satisfy the need without ever reaching satisfaction."

Of all the human feelings, gratitude has the shortest memory.

If you can't be satisfied with what you've reached, be thankful for what you've escaped.

Cicero said, "A thankful heart is not only the greatest virtue, but the parent of all other virtues."

The degree that you are grateful is a sure index of your spiritual health.

Max Lucado wrote, "The devil doesn't have to steal anything from you, all he has to do is make you take it for granted." When you count all of your blessings, you will always show a profit.

Replace regret with gratitude.

Be grateful for what you have, not regretful for what you have not.

The Bible says in Psalm 95:2 , "Let us come before his presence with thanksgiving."

Henry Ward Beecher said, "The unthankful . . . discovers no mercies, but the appreciative heart . . . will find in every hour, some heavenly blessings."

The more you complain the less you'll obtain.

If you don't enjoy what you have, how could you be happier with more?

The seeds of discouragement will not grow in a grateful heart.

"If we get everything we want, we will soon want nothing that we get."

Vernon Luchies

Francis Schaeffer said, "The beginning of man's rebellion against God was, and is, the lack of a thankful heart."

Epicurus reflected, "Nothing is enough for a man to whom enough is too little."

It's a sure sign of mediocrity to be moderate with our thanks.

Don't find yourself so busy asking God for favors that you have no time to thank Him.

I believe we should have the attitude of George Hubert, when he said, "Thou O Lord has given so much to me, give me one more thing—a grateful heart."

I relate to what Joel Budd said: "I feel like I'm the one who wrote Amazing Grace."

"Happiness always looks small while you hold it in your hands, but let it go, and you learn at once how big and precious it is."

Maxim Gorky

Our thanks to God should always precede our requests of Him.

The Bible challenges us in 1 Thessalonians 5:17-18, "Pray without ceasing; in everything give thanks" (NKJV).

"We don't thank God for much he has given us. Our prayers are too often the beggar's prayer, the prayer that asks for something. We offer too few prayers of thanksgiving and of praise."

Robert Woods

Don't find yourself at the end of your life saying, "What a wonderful life I've had! I only wish I'd appreciated and realized it sooner."

CHAPTER 33

UNACCEPTANCE OF THE PRESENT CREATES A FUTURE.

Change. I hope this word doesn't scare you but, rather, inspires you. Christians of all people are best prepared for changes. We have the Holy Spirit and God's Word. The Lord promises to "guide us with His eye," His Word will be "a lamp unto my feet and a light unto my path," and His plans for us are "blessed not cursed, plans to give us a hope and a future."

Change is what it takes to move forward in life and also helps you get what you want.

Herbert Spencer said, "A living thing is distinguished from a dead thing by the multiplicity of the changes at any moment taking place in it."

Change is an evidence of life. It is impossible to grow without change.

Those who cannot change their minds cannot change anything.

The person who never changes his opinion, never corrects his mistakes.

The truth is, life is always at some turning point.

What people want is progress, if they can have it without change. Impossible! You must change and recognize that change is your greatest ally.

Be open to God's change in your plans.

You cannot become what you are destined to be by remaining what you are.

John Patterson said, "Only fools and dead men don't change their minds. Fools won't. Dead men can't."

How many things have you seen that change just in the past year?

When you change yourself, opportunities will change.

Consider what Thomas Watson, the founder of the IBM Corporation, said, "There is a world market for about five computers." Now we have five computers in every house! Where would IBM be today if Mr. Watson had not been willing to change?

A traditionalist is simply a person whose mind is always open to new ideas, provided they are the same old ones.

Do not fear change, it is an unchangeable law of progress.

"There are people who not only strive to remain static themselves, but strive to keep everything else so . . . their position is almost laughably hopeless."

Odell Shepard

Wise people sometimes change their minds—fools, never.

The fact is, the road to success is always under construction.

Yesterday's formula for success is often tomorrow's recipe for failure.

The man who uses yesterday's methods in today's world won't be in business tomorrow.

Nothing's as permanent as change.

Apollo astronaut James Irwin said, "you might think going to the moon was the most scientific project ever, but they literally 'threw' us in the direction of the moon. We had to adjust our course every ten minutes, and we landed only inside fifty feet of our 500-mile radius of our target." Life, like this trip to the moon, is full of change and adjustments.

Mignon McLaughlin said, "It's the most unhappy people who most fear change."

When patterns and tradition break, new opportunities come together.

The same kind of thinking that has brought you to where you are will not necessarily get you to where you want to go.

Sante Boeve discovered this truth: "There are people whose watch stops at a certain hour and who remain permanently at that age."

Change is not your enemy—it is your friend.

CHAPTER 34

EXPECT SOMETHING FROM NOTHING.

Children do a good job of believing the Bible exactly as it says. A mother was concerned about her kindergarten son walking to school. He didn't want his mother to walk with him, and she wanted to give him the feeling that he had some independence but yet know that he was safe.

So she had an idea of how to handle it. She asked a neighbor if she would please follow him to school in the mornings, staying at a distance, so he probably wouldn't notice her. She said that since she was up early with her toddler anyway, it would be a good way for them to get some exercise as well, so she agreed.

The next school day, the neighbor and her little girl set out following behind Timmy as he walked to school with another neighbor girl he knew. She did this for the whole week.

As the two kids walked and chatted, kicking stones and twigs, Timmy's little friend noticed the same lady was following them as she seemed to do every day all week. Finally, she said to Timmy, "Have you noticed that lady following us to school all week? Do you know her?"

Timmy nonchalantly replied, "Yeah, I know who she is."

The little girl said, "Well, who is she?"

"That's just Shirley Goodnest," Timmy replied, "and her daughter Marcy."

"Shirley Goodnest? Who is she and why is she following us?"

"Well," Timmy explained, "every night my Mum makes me say the 23rd Psalm with my prayers, 'cuz she worries about me so much. And in the Psalm, it says, 'Shirley Goodnest and Marcy shall follow me all the days of my life,' so I guess I'll just have to get used to it!"

I believe that the primary cause of unhappiness in the world today is a lack of faith.

"Faith is putting all your eggs in God's basket, then counting your blessings before they hatch" (Ramona Carol). And I might add, don't worry about Him dropping them.

Faith is the force of a full life.

There's nothing like child-like faith. So, what is faith? John Spaulding said, "Your faith is what you believe, not what you know."

Put faith to work when doubting would be easier.

Faith is the anchor of the soul, the stimulus to action and the incentive to achievement.

Dr. Alexis Carrel says, "It is faith, and not reason, which impels men to action . . . intelligence is content to point out the road, but never drives along it."

I agree with Blaise Pascal: "Faith is a sounder guide than reason. Reason can only go so far, but faith has no limits.

Corrie Ten Boom says, "Faith is like a radar that sees through the fog of the reality of things at a distance that the human eye cannot see."

Faith sees the invisible, believes the incredible and receives the impossible. The Bible challenges us in 2 Corinthians 5:7 to walk by faith and not by sight.

Indecision will paralyze the flow of your faith. Faith demands a decision before it can work. Every accomplishment great or small . . . starts with belief.

Nothing but faith can accurately guide your life.

Faith gives us the courage to face the present with confidence and the future with expectancy.

Faith releases the miraculous. It is a way to God's divine influence. I agree with Pastor Tommy Barnett: "Faith is simply when you bring God into the picture."

And, where do we meet God? "God meets us at the level we expect, not the level we hope."

Gordon Robinson

At times, faith believes what you see isn't so. That's why the Bible says in Hebrews, "Faith is the substance of things hoped for, the evidence of things not seen" (11:1, NKJV).

Faith will never abandon you; only you can abandon it.

It is usually not so much the greatness of our troubles as the littleness of our faith that causes us to stop or complain.

Obedience is God's method of provision for your life.

The act of faith God leads you to do, triggers divine resources.

Faith either moves mountains, or it will tunnel through them. Saint Augustine said, "Faith is to believe what we do not see, and the reward of this faith is to see what we believe."

Faith keeps the man who keeps the faith.

Listen to Franklin Roosevelt: "The only limit to our realization of tomorrow will be our doubt of today."

Obedience brings blessings. Delayed obedience is disobedience. Obedience means at once.

No one can live in doubt when he has prayed in faith.

J. F. Clarke said, "All the strength and force of man comes from his faith in things unseen. He who believes is strong; he who doubts is weak. Strong convictions precede great actions."

Faith is necessary to succeed at anything worthwhile.

George Spaulding said, "Life without faith in something is too narrow of space in which to live."

As your faith increases, you will find you no longer need to have a sense of control. Things will flow as God wills, and you will be able to flow with them to your great happiness and benefit.

Let us move forward with strong and active faith.

CHAPTER 35

THOSE WHO DARE, DO.

As a drought continued for what seemed an eternity, a small community of farmers was in a quandary as to what to do. Rain was important to keep their crops healthy and sustain the way of life of the townspeople.

As the problem became more acute, a local pastor called a prayer meeting to ask for rain. Many people arrived. The pastor greeted most of them as they filed into the sanctuary. As he walked to the front of the church to officially begin the meeting, he noticed most people were chatting across the aisles and socializing with friends. When he reached the front, his thoughts were on quieting the attendees and starting the meeting.

His eyes scanned the crowd as he asked for quiet. He noticed an eleven-year-old girl sitting quietly in the front row. Her face was beaming with excitement. Next to her, poised and ready for use, was a bright red umbrella. The little girl's beauty and innocence made the pastor smile as he realized how much faith she possessed. No one else in the congregation had brought an umbrella.

All came to pray for rain, but the little girl had come expecting God to answer . . . .

Expect God to answer.

All of the important battles we face will be waged within ourselves. Nothing great has ever been achieved except by those who dared believe God inside of them was superior to any circumstance.

1 John 4:4 says, "Greater is He who is in you than He who is in the world" (NASB).

"Don't wait for all the lights to be green before you leave the house."

Jim Stovall

Don't do anything that doesn't require faith and God's help.

G. C. Lichtenberg said, "Never undertake anything for which you wouldn't have the courage to ask the blessings of heaven."

Ed Cole focusing on faith said, "There are three levels of knowledge. God is for me. God is with me. God is in me."

Mary Lyon said, "Trust in God—and do something."

Psalm 56:9 reads, "When I cry unto thee, then shall mine enemies turn back; this I know; for God is for me."

God gave man an upright countenance to survey the heavens and look upward toward him.

Accept and acknowledge only those thoughts that contribute to your success, that line up with God's Word and His will for your life.

Wayne Gretsky is, arguably, the greatest hockey player in history. Asked about his secret for continuing to lead the national hockey league in goals year after year, Gretsky replied, "I skate to where the puck is going to be, not where it has been."

Dare to go further than you can see.

"Seek not to understand that you may believe, but believe that you may understand."

Saint Augustine

Too many people expect little from God, ask little, and therefore receive little and are content with little.

Sherwood Eddie said, "Faith is not trying to believe something regardless of the evidence; faith is daring to do something regardless of the consequences."

Those who dare, do; those who dare not, do not.

You have reached stagnation when all you ever exercise is caution.

Theodore Roosevelt said, "Far better it is to dare mighty things, to win glorious triumphs, even though checkered by failure than to rank with those poor spirits who neither enjoy much nor suffer much because they live in the great twilight that knows not victory or defeat."

One of the riskiest things you can do in life is to take too many precautions and never stepped out in faith.

The Bible says in Isaiah 1:19, "If you are willing and obedient, you shall eat the good of the land" (NKJV).

Isak Dineson said, "God made the world round so that we would never be able to see too far down the road."

Sometimes you must press ahead despite the pounding fear in your head that says, "Turn back."

I sincerely believe that we would accomplish many more things if we did not so automatically view them as impossible.

If God is outside, something must be wrong inside.

Don't ever say conditions are not good. This limits God. If you wait for conditions to be exactly right, you will never obey God.

The person who dares for nothing need hope for nothing.

God will never allow anything to confront you that you and He together can't handle.

God said, "Come to the edge."
We said, "It's too high."
"Come to the edge."
We said, "We might fall."
"Come to the edge," God said.
And we came.
And he pushed us.
And we flew.

CHAPTER 36

WHAT YOU FEAR ABOUT TOMORROW IS NOT HERE YET.

A lot of people who are worrying about the future ought to be preparing for it.

Fear holds you back from flexing the risk muscle.

When you're robbed by worry, it's always an inside job.

Never take the advice of your fears. There is another way.

Things are rarely as they appear.

Never trouble trouble until trouble troubles you.

Arthur Roche said, "Worry is a thin stream of fear trickling through the mind. If encouraged, it cuts a channel into which all other thoughts are drained."

Worry seems to be the sin that most people are not afraid to commit.

We used to fear God. Now we fear everything else.

Nicholas Berdyaev says, "Victory over fear is the first spiritual duty of man."

Don't waste time in doubts and fears about what you don't have or might get.

Fears, like babies, increase larger by nursing them.

Fear wants to grow faster than teenagers.

Disraeli says, "Nothing in life is more remarkable than the unnecessary anxiety which we endure, and generally create ourselves."

We must act in spite of fear . . . not because of it.

If you are afraid to step up to the plate, you will never hit a home run.

Lucy Montgomery said, "It only seems as if you are doing something when you are worrying."

Worry doesn't help tomorrow's troubles, but it does ruin today's happiness.

"A day of worry is more exhausting than a day of work."

John Lubbock

When you worry about the future, there will soon be no future for you to worry about.

No matter how much a person dreads the future, he usually wants to be around to see it. The truth is; more people fret about the future than prepare for it.

Don't fear, for the Lord is with you. He will never leave you to face your challenges alone.

Instead, do what Dr. Rob Gilbert advised: "It's all right to have butterflies in your stomach. Just get them to fly in formation."

Only your mind can produce fear.

George Porter said, "Always be on guard against your imagination. How many lions it creates in our paths, and so easily! And we suffer so much if we do not turn a deaf ear to its tales and suggestions."

Worry never fixes anything. Instead, attack fear by taking action.

Shakespeare wrote, "Our doubts are traitors, and they make us lose what we oft might win, by fearing to attempt."

Jesus said, "Which of you by worrying can add one cubit to his stature?"

So I agree with Helen Keller: "It gives me a deep, comforting sense that things seen are temporal and things unseen are eternal."

Sister Mary Tricky said, "Fear is faith that it won't work out." The Bible says in Psalms, "God is our refuge and strength, a very present help in trouble. Therefore, we will not fear."

We choose our joys and our fears long before we experience them.

Fears lie and make us not go where we might have won. There are always two voices sounding in our ears—the voice of fear and the voice of faith. One is the clamor of the senses. The other is the whispering of God.

Never let your worries hold you back from pursuing your dream.

CHAPTER 37

EVERY MEDIOCRE PERSON
HAS GOOD INTENTIONS.

E. M. Bounds said, "There is neither encouragement nor room in Bible religion for feeble desires, listless efforts, lazy attitudes; all must be strenuous, urgent, ardent. Flamed desires, impassioned, unwary insistence delights heaven. God would have His children incorrigibly in earnest and persistently bold in their efforts."

When you are bold, His mighty powers will come to your aid.

If you want success, you must seize your opportunities as you go.

I agree with Jonathan Winters: "I couldn't wait for success—so I went ahead without it."

Lillian Hellman said, "It is best to act with confidence, no matter how little right you have to it."

George Adams said, "In this life we only get those things for which we hunt, for which we strive and for which we are willing to sacrifice."

Let me ask you the age-old question: "Are you waiting on God, or is He waiting on you?" I believe the vast majority of the time, He is waiting on us. Is God your hope or your excuse? I'm convinced He wants you to take the initiative, to live your life on the offensive. William Menninger said, "The amount of satisfaction you get from life depends largely on your ingenuity, self-sufficiency, and resourcefulness. People who wait around for life to supply their satisfaction usually find boredom instead."

Traveling around the United States and the world, I've seen a lot. Sometimes I find myself going back to the same place with the same people, with years separating the visits. Often a change in appearances is startling (I'm glad I've not aged). Sometimes it's not (lucky people). Every once in a while I meet someone stuck in exactly the same place as the last time I saw him or her. It's like they're in a time warp. Same problem, same excuses. Same story, same "no ending." And here's an absolute . . . they're always unhappy. There's a reason. They are doing, acting and being the same year after year. No wonder they're miserable and sad.

Albert Hubert remarked, "Parties who want milk should not seat themselves on a stool in the middle of the field and hope that the cow will back up to them."

Do like Sara Teasdale said: "I make the most of all that comes and the least of all that goes."

The door of opportunity won't open unless you push.

It is always a bumpy, uphill road that leads to heights of greatness.

Being on the defensive has never produced ultimate victory.

I believe that God helps the courageous.

One bold action is more valuable than 1,000 good intentions.

"Security is mostly a superstition. It does not exist in nature, nor do the children of men as a whole experience it. Avoiding danger is no safer in the long run than outright exposure. Life is either a daring adventure or nothing."

Helen Keller

Don't just face opportunities and problems, attack them.

Consider what B. C. Forbes said, "Mediocre men wait for opportunities to come to them. Strong, able, alert men go after opportunity."

Opportunities are all around you. Go after them.

CHAPTER 38

LAUNCH OUT!

A young boy's father was a horse trainer causing his family to move from stable to stable, from ranch to ranch, training horses. Thus, the boy's school career was constantly interrupted. One day, when he was a senior, a teacher asked him to write about what he wanted to be when he grew up. He did not hesitate a minute and wrote a seven-page paper about his aim to be an owner of a horse ranch; he wrote many details and drew a location of buildings and stables and even a detailed house plan.

Two days later he received his paper back with the letter "F" on the front page. After class, he came to the teacher and asked, "Why did I receive an F?"

The teacher responded, "This dream is so unrealistic for a boy like you, who has no money, no resources, and who comes from an itinerant family. There is no possibility that you will reach your great goals one day." Then the teacher offered him an opportunity to rewrite the paper with a more realistic conclusion.

The boy went home and asked his father how he should act. The father answered, "This decision is very important for you. So you have to make up your own mind on this."

After several days, the boy brought the same paper to his

teacher. No changes were made. He said, "You keep the F and I will keep my dream."

Today, that dreamer, Monty Roberts, lives in a beautiful home on a 200-acre horse ranch and has that original senior paper hanging over his fireplace.

Everyone loves something. We're shaped and motivated by what we love. It's our passion.

Ignore what you are passionate about, and you ignore one of the greatest potentials God has put inside you.

What gets your heart racing? What are you hungry to learn and know more? What do you daydream about doing? What captures your heart, your attention?

Life is too short to think small. Rather do as Joel Budd encourages us to do: "March off the map."

Most people could do more than they think they can, but they usually do less than they think they can.

I agree with Oscar Wilde when he said, "Moderation is a fatal thing. Nothing succeeds like excess."

Charles Schwab said, "When a man has put a limit on what he will do he has put a limit on what he can do."

Dr. J. A. Holmes said, "Never tell a young person that something cannot be done. God may have been waiting for centuries for somebody ignorant enough of the impossible to do that thing."

Say no to those who would hold you back and yes to the dream inside you.

If you devalue your dreams, rest assured the world won't raise the price.

You will find that great leaders are rarely "realistic" by other people's standards.

The answer to your future lies outside the confines that you have right now.

If you want to see if you can really swim, don't frustrate yourself with shallow water.

Cavett Robert said, "Any man who selects a goal in life which can be fully achieved has already defined his own limitations."

Other people may be smarter, better educated, or more experienced than you, but no single person has a corner on dreams, desire, or ambition.

Capture Randy Loescher's perspective: "God says, 'Ask me for the mountain.'"

Everything is possible—never use the word *never*.

Develop an infinite capacity to ignore what others think can't be done. Don't just grow where you are planted. Bloom where you are planted and bear fruit.

You never know what you cannot do until you try.

Rather be as Art Sepulveda said, "Be a history maker and a world shaker."

Go where you have never gone before.

Ronald McNair says, "You only become a winner if you are willing to walk over the edge."

The Bible says, "Things which are impossible with men are possible with God" (Luke 18:27, NKJV).

Take the lid off. Know your limits, then ignore them.

Consider how many fantastic projects have miscarried because of small thinking or strangled in their birth by a cowardly imagination.

I like what Marabeau said. When he heard the word *impossible*, he responded, "Never let me hear that foolish word again."

The creation of a thousand forests of opportunity can spring forth from one small acorn of an idea.

We should observe the future and act before it occurs.

No one can predict to what heights you can soar.

The Bible says, "Where there is no vision the people perish" (Proverbs 29:18). That's not God's best for you.

Dissatisfaction and discouragement aren't a result of the absence of things but the absence of vision.

To believe an idea impossible is to make it so.

Not being a person of imagination causes your life to be less than it was intended to be.

"No man that does not see visions will ever realize any high hope or undertake any high enterprise," said Woodrow Wilson.

Daniel Webster said, "There is always room at the top."

Even you will not know until you spread your wings.

When you climb the tallest tree, you win the right to the best fruit.

Gloria Swanson said, "Never say never. Never is a long, undependable thing, and life is too full of rich possibilities to have restrictions placed upon it."

Somebody is always doing what someone else says can't be done.

Pearl Buck said, "All things are possible until they are proved impossible—even the impossible may only be so as of now."

John Ruskin said, "Dream lofty dreams and as you dream, so you shall become. Your vision is the promise of what you shall at last unveil."

Spirella writes:
There is no thrill in easy sailing when skies are clear and blue,
There is no joy in merely doing things which any man can do.
But there is some satisfaction that is mighty sweet to take,
When you reach a destination that you thought you would never make.

CHAPTER 39

ADOPT THE VELOCITY OF GOD.

God's a God of timing and direction. He wants us to know what to do and when to do it.

Psalm 32:8 says, "I will instruct you and teach you in the way you should go; I will guide you with My eye" (NKJV).

Don't live your life ahead or outside of His will and way.

Beverly Sills says, "There are no shortcuts to any place worth going."

The way to the top is neither swift nor easy. Nothing worthwhile ever happens in a hurry—so be patient.

Because of impatience, we are driven out of God's will; continued impatience causes us not to return.

Don't be impatient: remember, you can't warm your hands by burning your fingers.

The Bible says, "Thy Word is a lamp unto my feet, and a light unto my path" (Psalm 119:105).

The less patience a person has the more he loses it.

God did not create rush.

Lord Chesterfield said, "Whoever is in a hurry shows that the thing he is about is too big for him."

Haste makes waste; give time time.

When you are outside of the right timing, you plant rushing and harvest frustration.

There is more to life than increasing its speed.

People that rush through life get to the end of it quicker.

One cool judgment is worth a thousand hasty conclusions.

Jumping to a wrong decision seldom leads to a happy landing.

Too many people leave the right opportunity to look for other opportunities.

Don't hurry when success depends on accuracy.

Those who make the worst use of their time are the first to complain of its shortness.

The fastest running back is useless unless heading toward the right goal line.

Brendon Francis commented, "Failure at a task may be the result of having tackled it at the wrong time."

Your success has little to do with speed, but much to do with timing and direction.

If the time has passed, preparation does no good.

Leonardo says, "Time stays long enough for anyone who will use it."

The trouble with life in the fast lane is that you get to the other end too soon.

Søren Kierkegaard said, "Most men pursue pleasure with such breathless haste that they hurry past it."

Many people overestimate what they can do in a year and underestimate what they can do in a lifetime.

What benefit is running if you're on the wrong road?

The key is doing the right thing at the right time.

Tryon Edwards said, "Have a time and place for everything, and do everything in its time and place, and you will not only accomplish more, but have far more leisure than those who are always hurrying."

The problem is that many a go-getter never stops long enough to let an opportunity catch up with him.

What good is aim if you don't know when to pull the trigger?

Ideas won't keep . . . something must be done about them.

"There is one thing stronger than all the armies in the world, and that is an idea whose time has come," says Victor Hugo.

Let God be your guide, and you will miss all the wrong places.

Bruyere said, "There is no road too long to the man who advances deliberately and without undue haste; no honor is too distant to the man who prepares himself for them with patience."

Many times the action that you take at the right time has no immediate relationship to the answer—it's to get you to the right place at the right time.

If you are facing the right direction, just keep on walking.

We are happiest when we discover that what we should be doing and what we are doing are the same things.

You will never be what you ought to be until you are doing what you ought to be doing.

Francis Bacon says, "The lame man who keeps the right road outstrips the runner who takes a wrong one . . . the more active and swift the latter is the further he will go astray."

Adopt the right pace: if you go too fast, you will catch up with misfortune. If you go too slowly, misfortune will catch up with you.

CHAPTER 40

MIRACLES BEGIN IN YOUR HEART.

Kids are great examples to us of having a good heart even if they miss the mark sometimes. One morning, the grandmother was surprised by her seven-year-old grandson. He had made her coffee. She drank what was the worst cup of coffee in her life. When she got to the bottom, there were three of those little green army men in the cup. She said, "Honey, what are the army men doing in my coffee?" Her grandson said, "Grandma, it says on TV 'The best part of waking up is soldiers in your cup!'"

The weapon of the brave resides in their heart.

When confronted with a new opportunity or challenging situation, I usually ask myself, "Do I have a pure heart and a right spirit?"

Psalm 139:23-24 prays, "Search me, O God, and know my heart: try me, and know my thoughts: and see if there be any wicked way in me, and lead me in the way everlasting."

Remember this: when you don't have the strength within, you won't have respect without.

You must first be a believer then an achiever.

"There are many things that will catch my eye, but there are only a very few that catch my heart . . . it is those I consider to pursue."

Tim Redmond

Horace Rutledge said, "When you look at the world in a narrow way, how mean it is! When you look at it selfishly, how selfish it is! But when you look at it in a broad, generous, friendly spirit, how wonderful you find it!"

The Bible counsels us to prove all things, holding fast to those which are good (1 Thessalonians 5:21).

God plants no yearning in your heart He doesn't plan to satisfy.

Sadly, we distrust our heart too much, and our head not enough.

Roger Babson added, "If things are not going well with you, begin your effort at correcting the situation by carefully examining the service you are rendering and especially the spirit in which you are rendering it."

What you set your heart on will determine how you spend your life.

2 Chronicles 16:9: "For the eyes of the LORD run to and fro throughout the whole earth, to shew himself strong in the behalf of them whose heart is perfect toward him."

Margaret Mitchell spoke this truth: "There ain't nothing from the outside that can lick any of us." James Allen added, "You will become as small as your controlling desire; as great as your dominant aspiration."

To know what is right and not do it is as bad as doing wrong.

God responds to pure hearts.

So, be moved by conviction, not ego.

"Learning to praise God after the answer is obedience. Learning to praise God before the answer is faith. Obedience is good, but faith moves God."

Bob Harrison

Faith builds a bridge from this world to the next.

Your eyes look for opportunity, your ears listen for direction, your mind requires a challenge and your heart longs for God's way.

Your heart has eyes that the brain knows nothing about.

William Hazlitt remarked, "If mankind would wish for what is right, they might have had it long ago."

Invite trouble and it will show up early.

Save yourself a lot of trouble by not borrowing any.

Here's more insight about trouble: you don't have to get rid of old problems to make room for new ones.

Nothing costs more than doing the wrong thing.

The man who borrows trouble is always in debt.

A person who persists in courting trouble will soon be married to it.

Before you can go high you must first go deep.

Keep your head and heart going in the right direction, and you won't have to worry about your feet.

CHAPTER 41

YOU CAN NEVER DEPEND UPON GOD TOO MUCH.

Anyone who doesn't believe in miracles is not a realist. Look around; nothing is more real than miracles.

When you leave God out, you'll find yourself without any invisible means of support.

Nothing great is achieved except by those who dared to believe that God inside them was superior to any circumstance.

Many people believe in God, but not many believe God.

One of the most incredible places we can live our lives is in a continual position of believing God.

"God made us, and God is able to empower us to do whatever He calls us to do. Denying we can accomplish God's work is not humility; it is the worst kind of pride."

Warren Wiersbe

The man who puts God first will find God with him right up to the last.

"In everything you do, put God first, and he will direct you and crown your efforts with success."

Proverbs 3:6, TLB

Unless it includes trusting God, it's not worthy of being called His direction.

Every divine direction we receive from God includes Him.

Never undertake anything for which you wouldn't have the conviction to ask the blessing of heaven.

"God never made a promise that was too good to be true."

D. L. Moody

One of the great things about believing God is in Luke 18:27: "The things which are impossible with men are possible with God."

What's possible is our highest responsibility.

When you join with Him in His plan, things that were impossible now become possible.

All great things have God involved in them.

If you put a buzzard in a pen six or eight feet square and entirely open at the top, the bird, in spite of his ability to fly, will be an absolute prisoner. The reason is that a buzzard always begins a flight from the ground with a run of ten or twelve feet. Without the space to run, as is his habit, he will not even attempt to fly but will remain a prisoner for life in a small jail with no top.

A bumblebee if dropped into an open tumbler will be there until it dies, unless it is taken out. It never sees the means of escape at the top but persists in trying to find some way out through the sides near the bottom. It will seek a way where none exists until it completely destroys itself.

Don't be like the buzzard and the bee. Struggling with problems and frustrations, not realizing your answer is right there above you.

If you dream big, believe big and pray big, do you know what happens? Big things!

Most of the things worth doing in history had seemed impossible before they attempted.

I just cannot understand how someone can't believe in God. You can see God everywhere if you just look.

You've never tapped God's resources until you have attempted the impossible.

The superior man seeks success in God. The small man seeks success in himself.

Joshua 1:9 also says, "Yes, be bold and strong! Banish fear and doubt! For remember, the Lord your God is with you wherever you go" (TLB).

The way each day will look to you all starts with whom you're looking to. Look to God. Believe God. When you believe God, you will see an opportunity in every problem, not problems in the middle of every opportunity.

Proverbs 16:3 is true when it says, "Commit to the Lord whatever you do, and your plans will succeed" (NIV).

Dare to go with God farther than you can see right now.

If something is beneficial for you, God will put it within your reach. One psalm in the Bible says, "No good thing will He withhold from those who walk uprightly" (Psalm 84:11, NKJV).

"I trust that God is on our side. But, it is more important to know that we are on God's side."

Abraham Lincoln

CHAPTER 42

GOD CAN.

Is God finished with you? If you're still breathing the answer is no. Don't die until you're dead. Psalm 138:8 says, "The Lord will perfect that which concerns me" (NKJV). God is continually developing and fine-tuning each of us. He wants to fulfill all of His promises and purposes in our lives.

God begins with a positive and ends with a positive. "Being confident of this very thing, that he which hath begun a good work in you will perform it until the day of Jesus Christ." Jesus hasn't come back yet, so that means God isn't finished with you. God's will for us is momentum, building on one good work to another.

As I've studied and known many godly leaders, I've found at crucial times they have said, "God led me to do . . ." Obedience to God's will is the GPS on the road to His plan for you. Never let anyone talk you out of pursuing a God-given idea. "Don't let someone else create your world for you, for when they do they always make it too small," said Ed Cole. Who's creating your world?

Oswald Chambers advises us: "Get into the habit of dealing with God about everything. Unless in the first waking moment of the day you learn to fling the door wide back and let God in, you will work on a wrong level all day; but swing the door wide open and pray to your Father in secret, and every public thing will be stamped with the presence of God."

Don't pray by heart but with the heart.

Billy Joe Daugherty said, "God is not hard to find! But there is a condition . . . we must seek Him with all our heart."

You will always get into trouble when you try to manage your life without God.

2 Chronicles 32:8 reads: "With us is the Lord our God, to help us and to fight our battles" (NKJV).

God, the ultimate warrior, lives in you.

If you are a soldier for Christ, don't worry about public opinion. Only be concerned about your Commander's opinion.

If you fear God, there is no need to fear anything else.

I believe we should follow Mary Lyons advice: "Trust in God and do something."

Consider the words of W. H. Atken when he said, "Lord, take my lips and speak through them; take my mind and think through it; take my heart and set it on fire."

To increase value, get to know God.

Satan doesn't care what we worship, as long as we don't worship God.

Too many people ask the Lord to guide them, and then they grab the steering wheel.

Your relationship with God will last if He is first in your life.

Too many people want God's blessing, but they don't want Him.

When you lose God, it isn't God who is lost. Some people talk about finding God as if He could get lost. The Bible says, "Draw near to God and He will draw near to you" (James 4:8, NKJV).

Tommy Barnett reflected, "The deeper I dig, the deeper He digs."

Pray to God: "I want to be in your will, not in your way."

A person who merely samples the Word of God never acquires much of taste for it.

William Law added, "Nothing has separated us from God, but our own will, or rather our own will is our separation from God." "God sends no one away except those who are full of themselves" (D. L. Moody).

The Bible finds us where we are and with our permission takes us where we ought to go.

Other books were given to us for information, but the Bible was given to us for transformation.

Consider this unique version of Psalm 35:27: "God is always a plus factor. He is never a disadvantage to you. He is always an asset. He wants you to succeed, and He has pleasure in the prosperity of His servant."

Our heartfelt cry to God ought to be the same as Isaiah's cry: "Here am I. Send me!" (Isaiah 6:8).

We must not only give what we have; we must also give what we are to God.

When God is all you have, then He is all you need.

ABOUT THE AUTHOR

John Mason is a national best-selling author, minister, executive author coach and noted speaker. He's the founder and president of Insight International and Insight Publishing Group—organizations dedicated to helping people reach their dreams and fulfill their God-given destiny.

He has authored fourteen books including *An Enemy Called Average, You're Born An Original—Don't Die A Copy, Let Go of Whatever Makes You Stop,* and *Know Your Limits—Then Ignore Them,* which have sold over 1.6 million copies and are translated into thirty-eight languages throughout the world. His books are widely respected as a source of godly wisdom, scriptural motivation and practical principles. His writings have been published in *Reader's Digest* along with numerous other national publications, and five of his books have reached the number-one spot on Amazon best-seller lists.

Known for his quick wit, powerful thoughts and insightful ideas, he is a popular speaker across the U.S. and around the world.

John and his wife Linda have four children: Michelle, Greg, Michael and David. They reside in Tulsa, Oklahoma.

WORTHY®
Inspired

If you enjoyed this book, will you consider sharing
the message with others?

- Mention the book in a Facebook post, Twitter update,
  Pinterest pin, blog post, or upload a picture through
  Instagram.
- Recommend this book to those in your small group,
  book club, workplace, and classes.
- Head over to facebook.com/worthypublishing, "LIKE"
  the page, and post a comment as to what you enjoyed
  the most.
- Pick up a copy for someone you know who would be
  challenged and encouraged by this message.
- Write a book review online.

You can subscribe to Worthy Publishing's
newsletter at worthypublishing.com.

Worthy Publishing Facebook Page   Worthy Publishing Website